POWER UP

A PRACTICAL HANDBOOK FOR TEACHERS

Bruce Robertson

Formative assessment | Responsive teaching | Pedagogical coaching

Your Questioning

hachette LEARNING

Although every effort has been made to ensure that website addresses are correct at time of going to press, Hachette Learning cannot be held responsible for the content of any website mentioned in this book. It is sometimes possible to find a relocated web page by typing in the address of the home page for a website in the URL window of your browser.

Hachette UK's policy is to use papers that are natural, renewable and recyclable products and made from wood grown in well-managed forests and other controlled sources. The logging and manufacturing processes are expected to conform to the environmental regulations of the country of origin.

To order, please visit www.HachetteLearning.com or contact Customer Service at education@hachette.co.uk / +44 (0)1235 827827.

ISBN: 978 1 0360 0317 3

© Bruce Robertson 2025

First published in 2025 by
Hachette Learning,
An Hachette UK Company
Carmelite House
50 Victoria Embankment
London EC4Y 0DZ

www.HachetteLearning.com

The authorised representative in the EEA is Hachette Ireland, 8 Castlecourt Centre, Dublin 15, D15 XTP3, Ireland (email: info@hbgi.ie).

Impression number   10 9 8 7 6 5 4 3 2

Year   2029 2028 2027 2026 2025

All rights reserved. Apart from any use permitted under UK copyright law, no part of this publication may be reproduced or transmitted in any form or by any means, electronic or mechanical, including photocopying and recording, or held within any information storage and retrieval system, without permission in writing from the publisher or under licence from the Copyright Licensing Agency Limited. Further details of such licences (for reprographic reproduction) may be obtained from the Copyright Licensing Agency Limited, www.cla.co.uk

Typeset in the UK.

Printed in Spain.

A catalogue record for this title is available from the British Library.

No matter how good you get, you can always get better, and that's the exciting part.
Tiger Woods

Bruce Robertson is the director of Next Level Educational, which focuses on high-quality professional development for teachers and school leaders. His books include *The Teaching Delusion* trilogy and *Power Up Your Pedagogy: The Illustrated Handbook of Teaching*, published by John Catt Educational. Of *Power Up Your Pedagogy*, Professor Rob Coe of Evidence Based Education says: 'To all teachers I would say: study this book, learn from it and act on it.' Bruce has been working in education for over 20 years, having trained as a chemistry teacher at The University of Edinburgh in 2002.

As headteacher, Bruce's leadership of Berwickshire High School from 2020–24 has been instrumental in turning around a school rated 'weak' and 'unsatisfactory' in an HMIE inspection, to one now widely recognised as sector-leading in its approaches to teaching and learning improvement, ethos and staff professional development. As a consultant and trainer, Bruce is widely praised for his passion, clarity and the practicality of his messages.

To my grandparents, Bruce and Jean.

Testimonials

This is another great book from Bruce Robertson, this time on the subject of questioning – something most teachers do most lessons, but which almost every teacher could learn to do even better. Bruce combines a deep understanding of the underlying research evidence, a close familiarity with everyday classroom practice, and the ability to distil what is actionable into concise, clear language. This combination is, to use his own words, genuinely powerful. I love the 'common pitfalls': truly widespread practices that misunderstand research-based advice or are less good than they could be. And the 'trusted techniques': simple (but robustly justified) practices that every teacher can learn. Every CPD library should include this book, and every teacher should read it!

Professor Rob Coe, director of research and development, Evidence Based Education

Robertson has done it again: *Power Up Your Pedagogy*, and now *Power Up Your Questioning*. Questioning is a cornerstone of impactful teaching, and this book offers insights and techniques about the art and science of effective questioning, leading to students thinking more critically, learning more collaboratively, and developing content and problem-solving thinking skills – as well as teachers responding more effectively to student questions and answers. An enticing format, a dynamism of flow throughout the book, and a worthwhile addition to the teacher toolkit.

John Hattie, laureate professor emeritus at The University of Melbourne, and author of Visible Learning *and* Visible Learning for Teachers

Power Up Your Questioning offers a masterclass in transforming classroom questioning into a powerful tool for learning. Combining practical strategies with cutting-edge insights from cognitive science, this book equips teachers to engage students, initiate critical thinking, and check understanding with precision. Whether you're a seasoned professional or new to the classroom, this invaluable guide will elevate your teaching practice and help you unlock the full potential of your students' thinking.

Dr Carl Hendrick, Academica University of Applied Sciences

Bruce Robertson's eloquent new book is strongly grounded in professional expertise and in the best research on how students learn. It can inspire the work of all teachers – in school, college or university. And it should be read by policymakers for advice on how to improve learning by students of all backgrounds, interests and abilities.

Lindsay Paterson, professor emeritus of education policy, Edinburgh University

Teachers ask questions every lesson, every day and multiple times within a lesson! Therefore questioning should be a central focus of pedagogy, planning and professional development, but it has not always received the attention it deserves. *Power Up Your Questioning* by Bruce Robertson is superb and guaranteed to help classroom teachers from those early in their career to more experienced teachers. It will also be very useful for leaders at all levels. As shown in this book, if we want better answers from the learners in front of us, we have to ask better questions. I wholeheartedly recommend this book; it will have a very positive impact on those that read it, reflect on it and act on it.

Kate Jones, senior associate for teaching and learning at Evidence Based Education and best-selling author

'Questions create thinking conditions, which means they create learning conditions.'

This brilliant book by Bruce Robertson shows us just how this is done. He masterfully weaves the evidence-informed ideas of edu-greats into pedagogy that teachers can incorporate into daily practices and discusses '20 key messages that *all* teachers and school leaders really need to know'. Robertson translates these key messages into actionable steps that provide insight into common pitfalls, power-up prompts, deeper-thinking questions, and trusted techniques. Furthermore, he gives us 10 recommended steps to get the most out of the book; it is as if he hands us a lesson plan to ensure that the 'quality of our questions promote desirable thinking' through the use of self-reflection and coaching.

Robertson states, 'Becoming a questioning expert takes years of deliberate practice and refinement.' *Power Up Your Questioning* not only speeds up the process of becoming a questioning expert, but it also stands as a reminder for experienced teachers, a blueprint for coaches, observable techniques for leaders, and most importantly, an avenue of lasting learning for our students.

'Great teaching ... is about eliciting rigorous evidence of where students are in their learning and responding accordingly.' Bruce Robertson artfully elicits evidence of where *we* are as teachers and guides us accordingly to become powerful questioning experts.

Patrice Bain, Ed.S. K–12, university educator, speaker, and co-author of the US Department of Education's guide Organizing Instruction and Study to Improve Student Learning *and* Powerful Teaching: Unleash the Science of Learning

Contents

Foreword 2

Why questioning? 7

Learning and how it happens: key messages all teachers and school leaders need to know 13

How to use this book 29

Power up your questioning 35
- **Theme 1** Asking more questions – *to create more opportunities for students to think* 35
- **Theme 2** Asking better questions – *to encourage desirable thinking* 47
- **Theme 3** Getting more students to think about each question – *so more students are learning* 75
- **Theme 4** Responding better to students' answers – *so you can explore their thinking and push learning forward* 103
- **Theme 5** Getting more students to learn from each other – *to enrich the learning experience for everyone* 141
- **Theme 6** Making time to check understanding and review learning – *so you can adjust your teaching accordingly* 161

Summary and further support resources 185
- Summary of how to use this book 186
- SURF: a framework to support pedagogical coaching conversations 188
- Pedagogical coaching conversation examples 189

Afterword: power up in every lesson, every week 193

References 194

Acknowledgements 196

Foreword

Whether teaching is a profession or not has been debated for decades. Some, such as John Gardner,[1] have suggested that it is at best a 'partial profession' since unlike professions like medicine and the law, there is no agreed knowledge base, there is no shared language of description, research evidence does not seem to cumulate, practitioners are not often involved in research, and so on.

However, there is one additional way that teaching is different from other professions and partial professions that gets little attention, and which has significant impact on practice. For most of us, in our first two decades of life, we have little involvement with doctors, lawyers, accountants and other professions, while we spend literally thousands of hours in schools. The result is that those of us involved in education learn much of what we know about teaching by the age of 18 – by being students.

This might not be so much of an issue if pre-service and in-service teacher education programmes spent a lot of time on the 'nuts and bolts' of teaching – such as the details of the difference between more effective and less effective feedback, the best ways to start lessons, how to manage classroom disruption and so on – but the evidence is that these fine-grained issues get relatively little attention. What this means is our models of what to do in classrooms are likely to be heavily influenced by our own experiences as students.

This is particularly marked in the area of questioning. Most teachers would agree that questioning is a central aspect of effective practice, but exactly how to do it is left to the teacher to figure out for themselves. It seems unlikely that anyone would be happy if surgeons were trained to remove the appendix by being told simply to make an incision in the abdomen, locate the appendix, remove it, and

---

1   Gardner, J. (2007) 'Is teaching a "partial" profession?' *Make the Grade: Journal of the Chartered Institute of Educational Assessors*, 2(Summer), 18–21.

then sew up the opening, and yet the advice given to most teachers is at this level of generality. This is a problem because in teaching, as in many other things, the tiniest details often matter a great deal.

A small but telling example is where we put a student's name in a question. If we ask, 'Bruce, what is the definition of a prime number?' then Bruce may well be the only one thinking about the answer. If on the other hand, we ask, 'What is the definition of a prime number?' and then wait a few seconds before asking for a response from Bruce, then many more of the class are likely to be thinking about the question.

Teachers are often told that open questions are better than closed questions, but this is often misleading, or straight-up incorrect. If the teacher knows of a specific misconception that students are likely to have, then a question such as 'Would your mass be the same on the moon?' can be useful even if it is about as closed as a question can get. After all, there are only two answers, and one of them is wrong. But it is worth asking because many students have not understood the distinction that physicists make between mass and weight. One could engage in an extended discussion with a student, hoping they might let slip that they believe that one's mass would be less on the moon than on Earth, but it is far more effective just to ask the question.

As well as being effective ways of identifying misconceptions, closed questions can also cause students to think. For example, we might ask students whether a square is a trapezium. Since most students are unlikely to have thought about this, it is likely to generate useful and purposeful discussion, even though, again, it is a closed question, with just two responses, one of which is incorrect.

In fact, whether a question is closed or open does not just depend on the question itself, but also on the 'classroom contract' the teacher has established with the students. If the teacher asks, 'What colour is the sky?' in some classrooms, every student would answer, 'Blue,' while in others, students would be striving to come up with ever more exotic descriptions such as 'turquoise', 'teal', and so on. In a similar vein, the question 'What do three threes make?' would elicit a single response, while in others, I have seen children respond with 'three hundred and thirty-three', 'a small flock of birds', and even 'a flower'.

In their pre-service education, teachers often also learn about lower-order and higher-order questions, if only to be told that teachers ask far more lower-order questions than higher-order ones. One study discussed by Brown and Wragg[2] found that teachers asked five times as many lower-order questions such as 'How many legs does an insect have?' as they did questions that required some thought rather than just factual recall. Teachers are typically told that higher-order questions are more important than lower-order ones, but this doesn't make much sense, because higher-order thinking requires knowledge. Even if we are primarily interested in our students' ability to answer higher-order questions, it is generally a good idea to check whether our students have the lower-order knowledge needed to engage in higher-order thinking. In order to understand the importance of the Treaty of London to the establishment of sustainable communities in the Americas in the early 17th century, it is necessary to know that the signing of the Treaty of London 1604 ended the long dispute between England and Spain, permitting supplies to reach the first permanent settlement in Jamestown, which was established in 1608.

I could go on, but I hope these examples serve to show how complex even apparently simple aspects of questioning can be, and how little input teachers get on the nuts and bolts of the practice, either in their initial training, or subsequently, in their continuing professional development. More importantly, every teacher can improve the way that they use questions, resulting in better information about pupil understanding, increasing engagement in the lesson, and strengthening students' understanding.

---

2   Brown, G. and Wragg, E. C. (1993) *Questioning*. London, UK: Routledge.

And that is why *Power Up Your Questioning* is such a useful and important contribution. By getting into the fine detail of questioning practice, Bruce Robertson provides a framework that allows any teacher to reflect productively on their current practice, and to explore ways of making their teaching even more effective. Whether you are a veteran with decades of classroom experience, or someone just beginning a career as a teacher, you will find much to think about, and many practical, immediately applicable ways to 'Power Up Your Questioning'.

Dylan Wiliam, UCL Institute of Education

Why questioning?

Why questioning?

Welcome to *Power Up Your Questioning: A Practical Handbook for Teachers*, a companion to *Power Up Your Pedagogy: The Illustrated Handbook of Teaching*.

Questioning is arguably one of the most important aspects of pedagogy a teacher can focus on developing, such is the impact it can have on students' learning. However, questioning is also one of the most challenging aspects of a teacher's job to master. It's one thing to ask questions; it's another to do this *really well*.

Becoming a **questioning expert** – which I would argue is a sensible goal for *all* teachers to pursue – takes years of deliberate practice and refinement. Even if a teacher has become 'expert' in this area, there is no limit to the improvements they can continue to make for as long as they are teaching. If this book does its job properly, it will support you to make your questioning *even better* than it is already, no matter how good that might be.

Why is questioning so important?

In a book that is devoted to the topic of questioning, it only seems appropriate to kick off early with a question. So, the first question for you to consider is: why is questioning so important? There are many reasons, but four of the most important can be summarised using the acronym **STAR**:

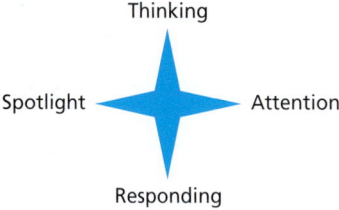

- **Spotlight**: Students' answers to questions shine a spotlight on the things they know and understand, or don't.
- **Thinking**: Questions make students think, and – as we shall go on to discuss – thinking is the key to learning.
- **Attention**: Questions help check and hold student attention, which is a prerequisite to learning.
- **Responding**: By making students' thinking and learning visible, questions provide teachers (and students) with invaluable formative information about what to do next. As a formative assessment tool, questioning is king.

We will refer to the STAR acronym later in this book during our exploration of different Trusted Techniques.

What does educational literature say?

Educational literature has a lot to say about the importance of questioning to learning. Let's highlight some key examples.

'Principles of instruction' – Barak Rosenshine

In 'Principles of instruction', Professor Barak Rosenshine suggests that the *most effective* teachers are ones who **ask a large number of questions** and **check the responses of all students**.[3] He elaborates:

> 'Students need to practice new material. The teacher's questions and student discussion are a major way of providing this necessary practice. The most successful teachers … [spend] more than half of the class time lecturing, demonstrating, and asking questions. Questions allow a teacher to determine how well the material has been learned and whether there is a need for additional

---

3 Rosenshine, B. (2012) 'Principles of instruction.'

instruction. The most effective teachers also ask students to explain the process they used to answer the question, to explain how the answer was found. Less successful teachers ask fewer questions and almost no process questions.'

'A Model for Great Teaching' – Evidence Based Education

Evidence Based Education's 'A Model for Great Teaching' suggests that '**activating hard thinking**' is one of the best things a teacher can do to help students' learning and highlights questioning as a key means to achieve this.[4] Effective teacher questioning is described as follows:

> 'Using questions and dialogue to promote elaboration and connected, flexible thinking among learners (e.g., 'Why?', 'Compare', etc.); using questions to elicit student thinking; getting responses from all students; using high-quality assessment to evidence learning; interpreting, communicating and responding to assessment evidence appropriately.'

Embedded Formative Assessment – Dylan Wiliam

The importance of questioning is highlighted throughout *Embedded Formative Assessment* by Professor Dylan Wiliam.[5] For example, Professor Wiliam highlights the importance of teachers using questions to **elicit evidence of learning**, so they are in a **position to provide feedback** to the learners about what to do next. He suggests that sharing high-quality questions (between different teachers and schools) may be the most significant thing we can do to improve the quality of student learning. Professor Wiliam also writes:

---

4   https://evidencebased.education/a-model-for-great-teaching/
5   Wiliam, D. (2011) *Embedded Formative Assessment.*

'Teachers must acknowledge that what their students learn is not necessarily what they intended, and this is inevitable because of the unpredictability of teaching. Thus, it is essential that teachers explore students' thinking before assuming that students have understood something.'

In other words, questioning plays an essential role in helping teachers to gauge the size of, and to close, the '**teaching–learning gap**':

Visible Learning for Teachers – John Hattie

In *Visible Learning for Teachers*, Professor John Hattie highlights questioning as having a relatively high effect size.[6] He suggests that the most important task for teachers is to listen and reminds us that listening requires dialogue, which questions help create. He also suggests that the most effective lessons tend to be those in which students' answers to questions are valued as the most important thing going on, such is their formative power. In other words, the lesson might be 'teacher-led', but it's actually the voices of students that are dominating.

Our list could go on, but I think you get the idea: high-quality questioning is a fundamental ingredient of great teaching. Mastering it requires skill, refinement and more than a little artistry, all of which this book is designed to support.

---

6   Hattie, J. (2012) *Visible Learning for Teachers*.

Learning and how it happens

Key messages all teachers and
school leaders need to know

Learning and how it happens
Key messages all teachers and school leaders need to know

The decisions teachers make about what to do – or not do – in lessons should be grounded in key messages from cognitive science about how learning happens and educational research about pedagogies that are most likely to be effective at particular times. The feedback teachers are offered by anyone who observes them teach should be grounded in the same key messages.

However, a major and often-glossed-over issue in the teaching profession is a lack of focus on such messages. To help address this, what follows is a summary of 20 key messages that *all* teachers and school leaders really need to know.[7] These are designed to **underpin pedagogical decision making** in lesson planning and delivery so that teachers feel empowered to make good decisions about what to do – and not do – in lessons, as opposed to simply doing (or not doing) something because they have been told to.[8] The better teachers and school leaders understand these messages, the better pedagogical decisions are likely to be, and the better conversations about lessons between teachers and school leaders are likely to be as well.

Working memory and long-term memory

Key message 1: It is helpful to think of our brains as having two memory compartments: **working memory** and **long-term memory**.[9]

---

[7] These apply to all learners, regardless of age and stage (Dylan Wiliam in discussion with Tom Sherrington and Emma Turner: www.youtube.com/watch?v=7ynsMwzsCsg). They also apply to all subject areas.
[8] Observation feedback such as 'don't talk for more than 10 minutes' – we're looking at you!
[9] Willingham, D.T. (2009) *Why Don't Students Like School?*

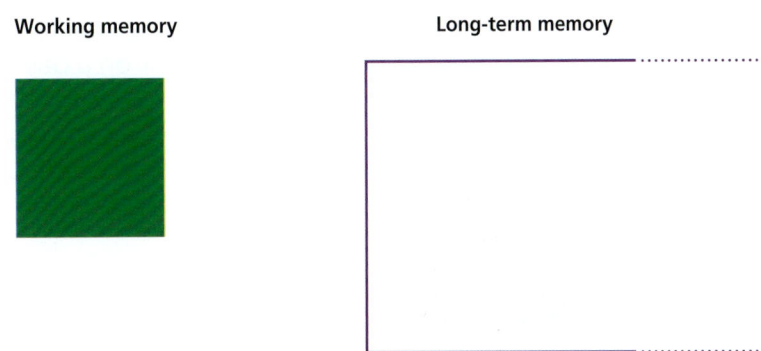

Key message 2: Whenever **information** comes to our attention (such as things that we see or hear, from presentations, books, videos, etc.), this enters working memory first.[10]

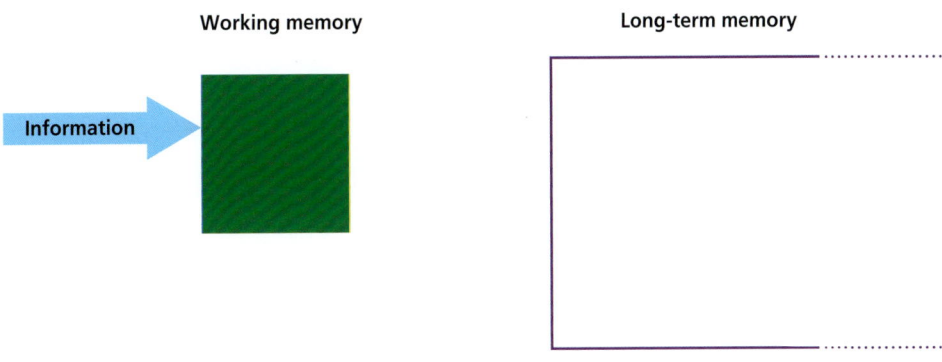

---

10   Willingham, D.T. (2009) *Why Don't Students Like School?*

Learning and how it happens

Key message 3: Working memory is limited by *how much* information it can hold and *how long* it can hold it.[11] For that reason, most of the information we see and hear on a day-to-day basis falls out of it relatively quickly.[12] In other words, it is **forgotten**.

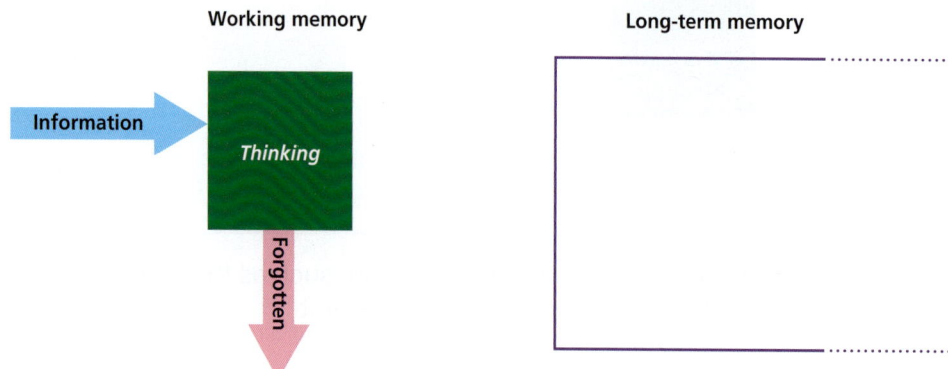

---

11 Kirschner, P.A. and Hendrick, C. (2020) *How Learning Happens*.
12 Brown, P.C., Roediger III, H.L. and McDaniel, M.A. (2014) *Make It Stick*.

Key message 4: However, not everything we see and hear falls out of working memory in this way. Sometimes, information *transfers* from working memory into long-term memory in a process called **encoding**.[13] Encoding is the first step to learning, which can be defined as **the development of long-term memory**.[14]

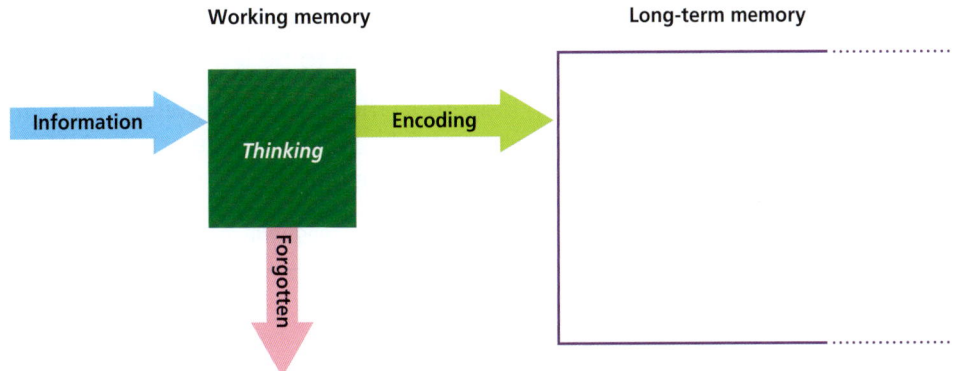

---

13 See, for example, Brown, P.C., Roediger III, H.L. and McDaniel, M.A. (2014) *Make It Stick*.
14 Robertson, B. (2020) *The Teaching Delusion*.

Thinking and storing

Key message 5: Working memory is the site of **thinking,** and the best way to get information to transfer from working memory to long-term memory is to think about it.[15] This is why Professor Daniel Willingham suggests that 'memory is the residue of thought'[16] and why the 'Great Teaching Toolkit' highlights 'activating hard thinking' as so important to effective teaching.[17] The more students think about something, and the harder they think about it, the more likely it is to be learned.[18]

Key message 6: Encoded information is stored in long-term memory as **knowledge**, of which there are two main types: *declarative knowledge* (of facts and concepts, which can be articulated) and *procedural knowledge* (of how to do things, which can't necessarily be articulated, but can be demonstrated).[19]

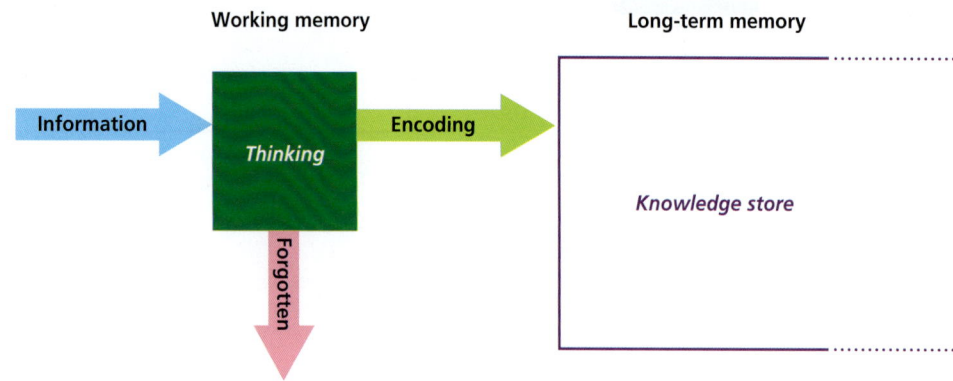

15 Brown, P.C., Roediger III, H.L. and McDaniel, M.A. (2014) *Make It Stick*.
16 Willingham, D.T. (2009) *Why Don't Students Like School?*
17 Coe, R. et al. (2020) *Great Teaching Toolkit*.
18 Brown, P.C., Roediger III, H.L. and McDaniel, M.A. (2014) *Make It Stick*.
19 Kirschner, P.A. and Hendrick, C. (2020) *How Learning Happens*.

Understanding

Key message 7: Knowledge stored in long-term memory doesn't sit in isolation. Rather, it exists in constructs called **schemata**.[20] In schemata, knowledge connects to related knowledge.[21] **Understanding** develops as knowledge connections get made. The more connections and the stronger these are, the more likely we are to both *understand* and *remember* something.[22]

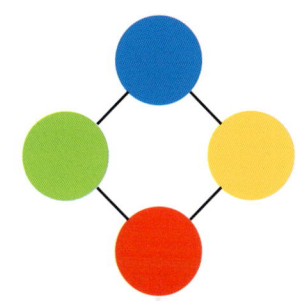

Making sense of new information

Key message 8: The reason we store knowledge in long-term memory is so we can *use it*. The most important thing we use it for is to *think with*.[23] As new information comes to our attention, we **retrieve** knowledge from long-term memory to make sense of it.[24] Sometimes, this is automatic; sometimes, it requires effort.

---

20 The singular is 'schema'.
21 https://sites.google.com/view/efratfurst/learning-in-the-brain
22 Brown, P.C., Roediger III, H.L. and McDaniel, M.A. (2014) *Make It Stick*.
23 Wiliam, D. (2018) *Creating the Schools Our Children Need*.
24 Kirschner, P.A. and Hendrick, C. (2020) *How Learning Happens*.

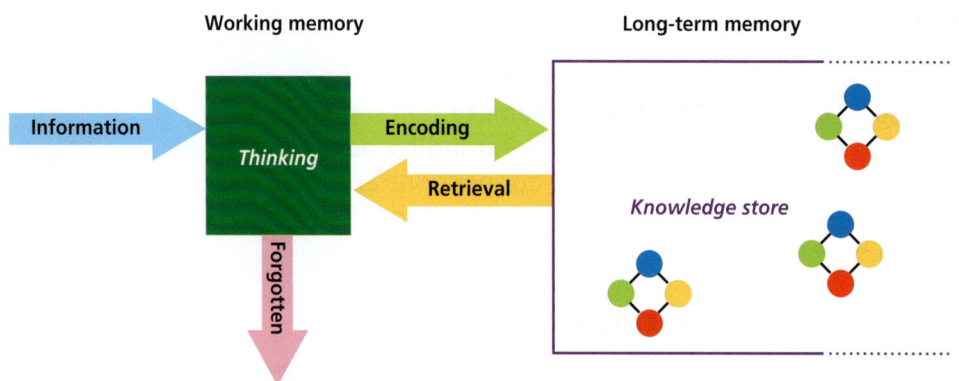

Key message 9: The extent to which we can make sense of, and think about, new information depends on the knowledge we have stored in long-term memory relating to this.[25] The more knowledge we have and the better organised this is, the more likely we are to understand something new and be able to think about it.

The effect of questions

Key message 10: **Questions promote knowledge retrieval and thinking**. For example, if you are asked to name a big cat with a mane, you will probably think 'lion'. You think that because you have pulled relevant knowledge from a schema in long-term memory into working memory. You weren't consciously aware of this knowledge until you were asked the question.[26]

---

25 Hirsch, E.D. (2016) *Why Knowledge Matters*.
26 Willingham, D.T. (2009) *Why Don't Students Like School?*

Schema activation

Key message 11: When one part of a schema is pulled from long-term memory into working memory, other parts are **activated** as well, making it more likely these will also be thought about.[27] For example, having started to think of a lion, you might also think about a jungle and other big cats.

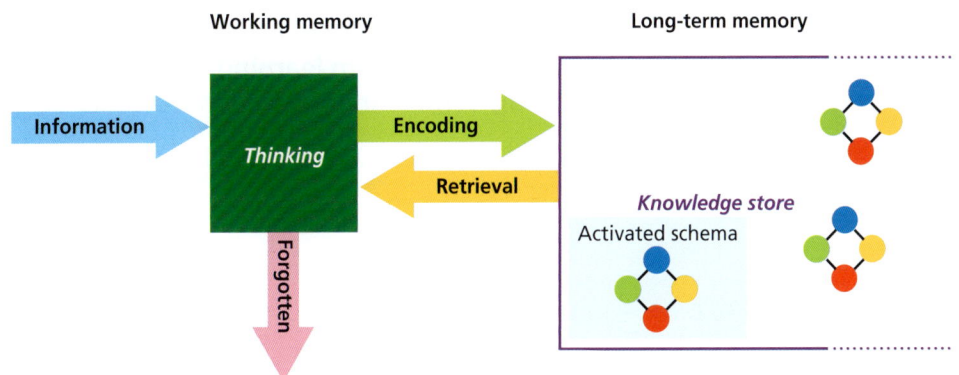

Key message 12: Activating a schema helps new things to be added to it. For example, if you want students to learn more about lions, it is probably a good idea to ask them a question on this topic *before* teaching new content. Effectively, their 'lions schema' becomes primed and ready to accommodate new knowledge.[28]

---

27 Kirschner, P.A. and Hendrick, C. (2020) *How Learning Happens*.
28 Mccrea, P. (2017) *Memorable Teaching*.

Learning and how it happens

Short-term learning vs long-term learning

Key message 13: Long-term memory is fluid. Over time, things that are stored there can change.[29] A common example of such change is **fading**, which results in memories becoming less easy to retrieve (even though they are still there). Fading explains why students often 'misremember' and 'forget' things, even if they have been 'taught' really well.[30] The key implication for teaching is that we can't assume that students will be able to do something in the future just because they are able to do it at the time they are taught.[31] In other words, there is a difference between **short-term learning** – which we could define as that which lasts minutes, hours, days or weeks – and **long-term learning** – which we could define as that which lasts months or years.

---

29 Willingham, D.T. (2009) *Why Don't Students Like School?*
30 'Taught' is in inverted commas because nothing has really been taught until it has been learned. This is a tough message for teachers but also an important one to accept.
31 Bjork, E.L. and Bjork, R.A. (2014) 'Making things hard on yourself, but in a good way.'

Key message 14: To conceptualise this, it can be helpful to think of long-term memory as having two sub-compartments: the **short-term knowledge store** and the **long-term knowledge store**:

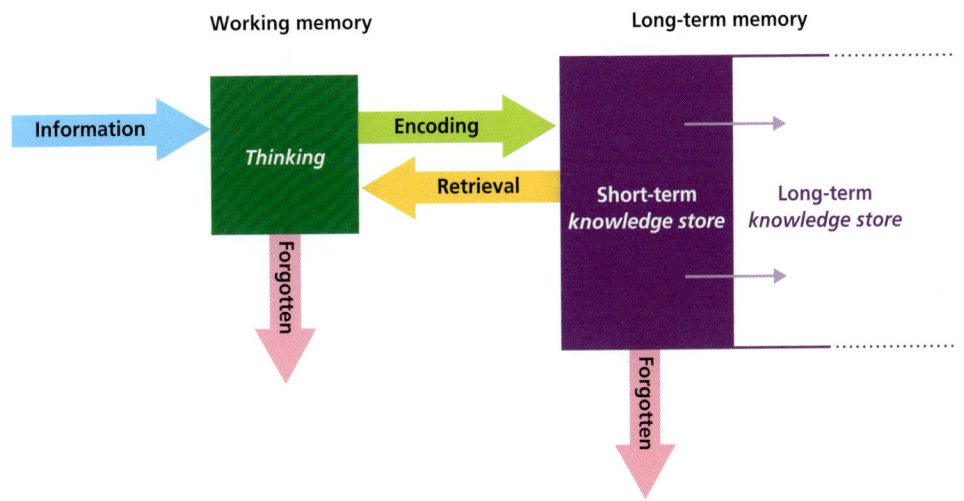

Whenever we start to learn anything new, it is the short-term knowledge store that will typically develop first. The goal of effective teaching is to ensure knowledge transfers from this area (where it can remain for minutes, hours, days or weeks) into the long-term knowledge store (where it can remain for months or, preferably, years).

Key message 15: The key principles relating to fading are captured neatly by the Ebbinghaus Forgetting Curve:[32]

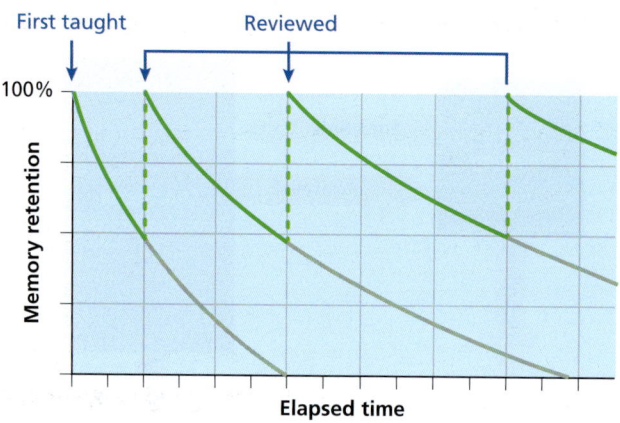

This shows that:
1 Fading tends to start almost immediately from the point something is first taught.
2 The effects of fading can be reversed if content is reviewed (bringing retention back to 100%).
3 The more content is reviewed, the stronger memories become, meaning the less quickly they fade and the easier they are to retrieve in future.

---

32 Shrestha, P. (2017) *Ebbinghaus Forgetting Curve*.

Reverse fading

Key message 16: A key aspect of a teacher's job is to address fading and undo it. The best way to do this is to get students to **think about the same material** in **spaced intervals** and in **a variety of ways**.

Key message 17: When students think about the same material, they revisit it in an *active way*. As memories are retrieved from long-term memory, they are strengthened according to a cognitive principle known as the testing effect: **retrieval strengthens memory**.[33] The act of pulling a memory from long-term memory makes it stronger. As a result, it is less likely to be forgotten.

An alternative way to frame this is that retrieval makes it more likely that knowledge will transfer from the *short-term knowledge store* of long-term memory to the *long-term knowledge store*. The key point for teachers is that *active revisiting*, which can be encouraged by asking questions, will almost always be better for students' learning than *passive revisiting*, such as students seeing, hearing or reading things again in a presentation, video or book, because these activities don't utilise the testing effect. When we talk about 'active learning', what we should have in mind is thinking and retrieval (rather than students being physically active, for no good reason).

---

33 Barton, C. (2018) *How I Wish I'd Taught Maths*.

Key message 18: If active revisits take place in spaced intervals, teaching can utilise the forgetting effect.[34] This effect suggests that, counterintuitively, **a little forgetting is good for learning**. If we allow memories to fade a little, so long as they haven't faded so much that they can't be retrieved (despite prompts), the impact of the testing effect will be greater than if the memory had been stronger in the first place.[35]

The key point for teachers is that knowledge retrieval is best for learning when the activities that require this are spaced out.

Key message 19: Encouraging students to think about things in **a variety of ways** helps to develop knowledge connections within and between schemata.[36] For example, if students are learning about the anatomy of the heart, they might be asked to:

- Label a blank diagram
- Correct the deliberate mistakes in a prelabelled diagram
- Describe the structure of the heart to a partner from memory.

---

34 This is also often referred to as the spacing effect.
35 Bjork, E.L. and Bjork, R.A. (2014) 'Making things hard on yourself, but in a good way.'
36 Enser, Z. and Enser, M. (2020) *Fiorella & Mayer's Generative Learning in Action*.

The more connections that get made and the stronger these are, the less likely fading will happen and the more likely knowledge can be easily retrieved. In other words, the more connections that get made, the more likely it is that knowledge will move from the short-term knowledge store of long-term memory to the long-term knowledge store.

Key message 20: As a rule of thumb, **students typically need to think about things on at least three separate occasions before they are likely to be learned**.[37] While there are no absolutes as to what 'separate' means, a useful steer for teachers is to think about active reviews as short cycle (within the same lesson), medium cycle (after a few days) and long cycle (after a few weeks or months).[38] When teaching is at its most effective, there are planned opportunities for active reviews in all three cycles.

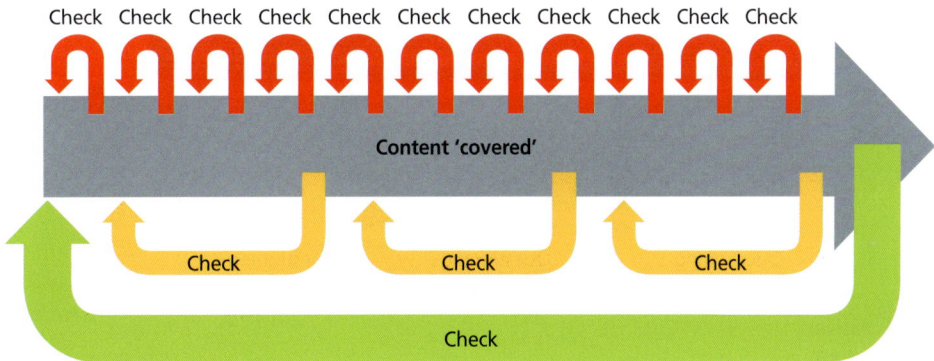

---

37 Nuthall, G. (2007) *The Hidden Lives of Learners*.
38 Adapted from Wiliam, D. (2018) *Creating the Schools Our Children Need*.

Learning and how it happens

The link to questioning

The key messages we have discussed in this section help to explain why questioning is so important in great teaching. Questioning helps drive the transfer of information/knowledge between working memory and long-term memory in both directions. It is a **catalyst for learning**. Questioning also helps to drive the actions of the teacher based on the formative information they glean from questioning. It is a **route map for responsive teaching**.

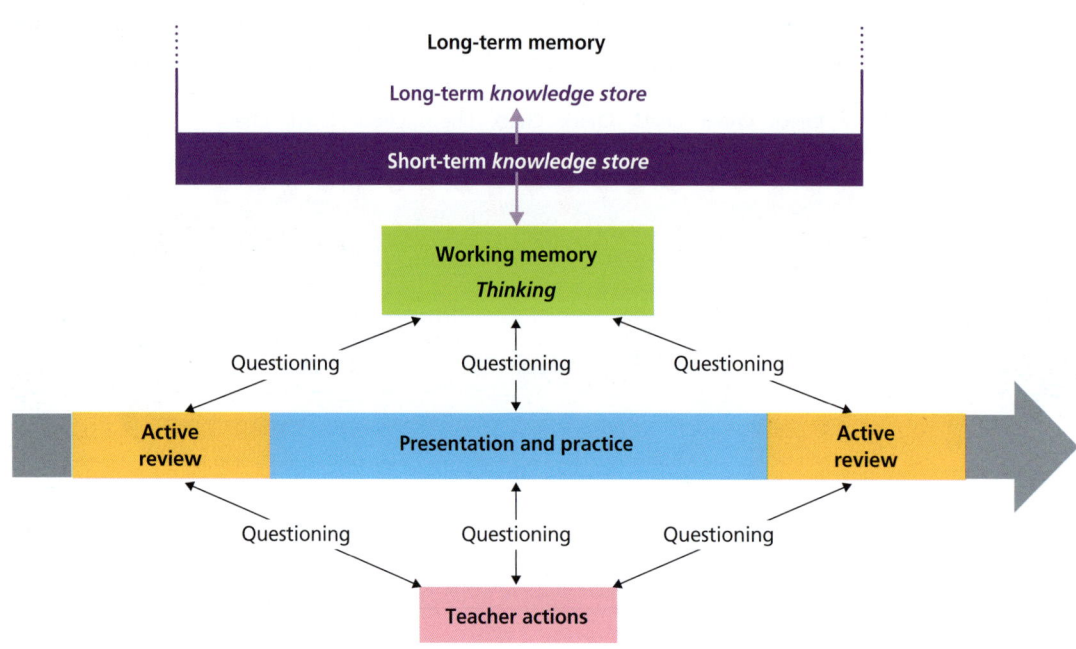

How to use this book

How to use this book

Where are we starting?

David Ausubel once said that the most important thing for a teacher to do is **find out where students are in their learning and teach them accordingly**.[39] With this in mind, I would like you to answer the following question: on a scale of 1–10, how good would you say your questioning is typically? Take a moment to consider that. Hazarding a guess, I'm going to bet you haven't chosen '1'. However, I don't believe you will have chosen '10' either.[40] Probably, like most teachers, you will have hedged your bets and gone with a score between 6 and 8.

The next question for you to consider is: why did you choose this number? In other words:

- What do you think you are good at already?
- What do you think could be improved?

Take a moment to consider these questions as well.

Where are we going?

As you considered your current questioning practice, you probably reflected on one or more of the following:

- **Question quantity and frequency** – how many questions you ask and how often you ask them
- **Question quality** – how good your questions are, both verbal and written
- **Questioning technique** – how you go about asking questions.

---

39 Ausubel, D., Novak, J. and Hanesian, H. (1978) *Educational Psychology: A Cognitive View.*
40 If you have, I'm not sure how much you're going to get from this book!

Themes

This book is going to explore all three of these areas using six themes:

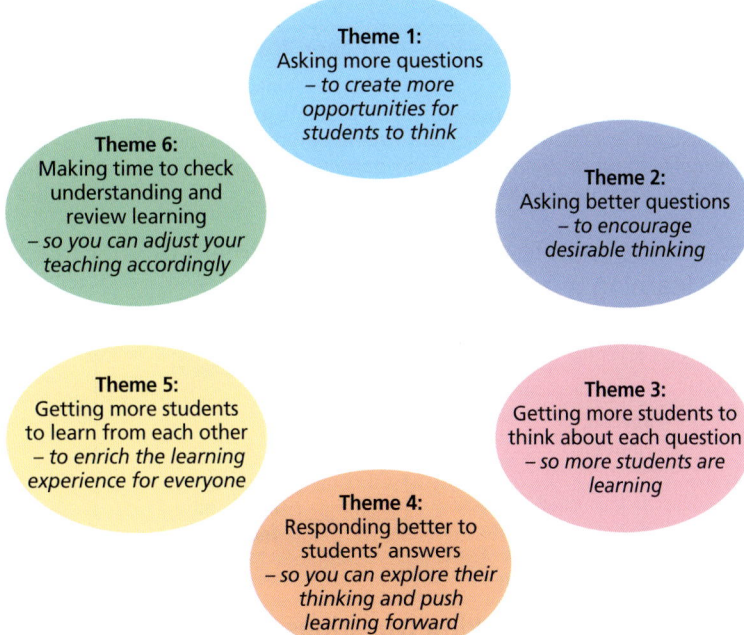

It's up to you if you want to work through these sequentially or pick a particular theme to start with. The advantage of reading this book sequentially is that we will often refer to things that were covered in an earlier theme.

Common Pitfalls, Power-Up Prompts, Deeper-Thinking Questions and Trusted Techniques

Each theme is divided into four sections:

Common Pitfalls	Power-Up Prompts	Deeper-Thinking Questions	Trusted Techniques
Common Pitfalls explore the 'traps' teachers often fall into with questioning and suggest ways these can be avoided.	Power-Up Prompts are statements that summarise key messages from a theme for you to think about or discuss, such as in coaching conversations.	Deeper-Thinking Questions are included to support further reflection or discussion of a particular theme.	Trusted Techniques are specific practices that you can focus on building into your teaching or getting (even) better at. There are 30 in total.

Collectively, these sections are designed to support the development of your teaching practice according to the following professional learning model:

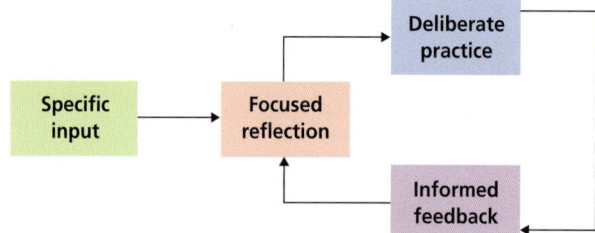

- The **Common Pitfalls** offer specific input.
- The **Power-Up Prompts** and **Deeper-Thinking Questions** support focused reflection.
- The **Trusted Techniques** are included to guide your deliberate practice.
- The only thing this book can't provide is a trusted colleague to offer informed feedback on your practice (so it's down to you or your school to set this up).

Power Up Your Questioning

As you work through the book, you will see this terminology in the footer of each page. This is to help signpost the main purpose of the section you are reading.

Ten recommended steps to get the most from this book

To get the most from this book, it is recommended that you follow 10 sequential steps:

1	Pick a theme...	...from one of the six explored.
2	Read...	...the **Common Pitfalls** relating to this theme.
3	Reflect...	...on your current practice using the **Power-Up Prompts** and **Deeper-Thinking Questions** to help guide your reflection.
4	Commit...	...to developing a specific aspect of your practice over the next 2-4 weeks, choosing one or more **Trusted Techniques** to focus on.[41]
5	Practise...	...this aspect in a deliberate way in every lesson over this period.
6	Revisit...	...the relevant sections of the book periodically to make sure you are on the right track.
7	Invite a colleague...	...to observe the aspect of practice you are working on at least once during the 2-4-week period. They don't have to observe a whole lesson – just a part relating to what you are working on.
8	Meet your colleague...	...to discuss their thoughts and suggestions. Use the **Common Pitfalls**, **Power-Up Prompts**, **Deeper-Thinking Questions** and/or **Trusted Techniques** sections to guide your discussion (choose the one you find the most useful).
9	Review...	...your progress and decide whether you have made sufficient improvements at the end of the 2-4-week period. ■ If you haven't, continue developing the aspect of practice you are currently working on. ■ If you have...
10	Choose another...	...aspect of practice to focus on. This might be from the same theme or a different one.

---

41 Not all techniques will work well on the first or second attempt. If you find that's the case, resist any temptation to give up. Many of the techniques take time and practice to master, and for students to get used to. Keep practising and revisit the details of the techniques in this book if you need to.

Steps 1–6 and 9–10 can be followed individually without the need to work with a colleague. Steps 7–8 focus on **pedagogical coaching** and require a colleague to work with. While you will get a lot from the book on your own using the first six and last two steps, you will get a *lot* more if you work with a colleague to follow steps 7–8 together using the pedagogical coaching approach outlined.

Now, having explained all of this, it's time to get going!

Power up your questioning

Theme 1: Asking more questions
– to create more opportunities for students to think

Overview

Common Pitfalls	Power-Up Prompts	Trusted Techniques
1. Believing that because you show or tell students something, they will learn it. 2. Not asking enough questions. 3. Talking for extended periods without asking a question.	Teacher exposition is infused with frequent questioning. - To what extent is this typically true? - What do you currently do to ensure this? - What could you do to make this even better?	More Questions, More Often

Common Pitfall 1: Believing that because you show or tell students something, they will learn it

As tempting as it is to believe students are learning new things as we present these to them, the reality is, many often aren't. The reason is because **exposure doesn't equal learning**.

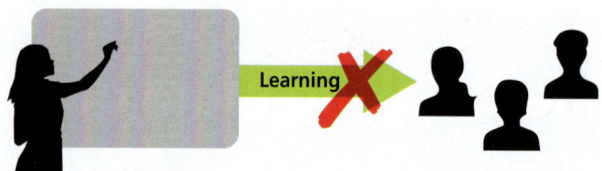

Showing and telling students things usually isn't enough for these to be learned – even if we do this *really well*. High-quality presentations, demonstrations, explanations and modelling will only get us so far. A crucial learning ingredient is missing.

What is the missing ingredient?

If we want students to *learn* specific things, we need to get them to *think* about specific things.[42] The more they think and the harder they do this, the more likely learning is to happen. Passive engagement (watching and listening without thinking) is not the same as active engagement (watching and listening while thinking). This is arguably the main reason why asking frequent questions is so important to effective teaching – questions create *thinking conditions*, which means they create *learning conditions*. The more questions we ask, the more students are likely to think, and so the more likely students are to learn.[43]

---

42 Willingham, D.T. (2009) *Why Don't Students Like School?*
43 Though, as we will go on to discuss in Theme 2, asking 'good' questions is as important as asking frequent questions.

> **Pitfall Avoidance Principle**
>
> As you plan and deliver presentations (explanations and demonstrations), focus on the importance of frequent questions as much as the quality of your resources and delivery.

Common Pitfall 2: Not asking enough questions

Do you ask enough questions?

Accepting the importance of thinking to learning and the key role that questions play, a logical question for you to ask yourself is 'do I ask enough questions?' To answer this, you first need to know how many questions you ask in a typical lesson so you can use this as a baseline.[44] *Do you know?* Most teachers don't, but it would probably be useful if they did. To find out, set yourself the goal of counting over a series of lessons and calculating the average. A clicker or a paper tally might help, or you could ask a student volunteer to help you.

Next, you need to determine how many questions you think would be an *optimal number* in a typical lesson. For the purposes of exemplification, let's imagine a 'typical lesson' lasts 45 minutes and includes a daily review, whole-class teaching, individual practice and a plenary review. It looks something like this:

Daily review	Whole-class teaching	Individual practice	Plenary review
5 minutes	20 minutes	15 minutes	5 minutes

---

44 Granted, all lessons are different. However, there does tend to be such a thing as a 'typical lesson' for individual teachers.

Specific input | Focused reflection | Deliberate practice

In a lesson taking this format, how many questions do you think you should be asking? You don't need to determine an exact number – a ballpark figure will do. Here are some options to choose from:

A Between 1 and 10

B Between 11 and 20

C Between 21 and 30

D Between 31 and 40

E More than 40.

Which would you pick?

Cards on the table, I would pick option **E**.[45] Let's explore this.

The dilemma of time

Most teachers agree that time is always the enemy in lessons. Frustratingly, there is no getting away from that. However, we can't let time pressures be an excuse not to teach in the best way possible. This means that we can't let time pressures get in the way of asking frequent questions, such is their importance to learning.

Different types of question

Accepting this, it should be helpful to draw a distinction between two different types of question: **targeted** and **follow-up**.

---

45 Some readers might gasp at this. If that's you, stick with me.

Targeted questions

A targeted question is any question that gets students to think about something specific. Sometimes, these require only knowledge retrieval (for example, 'In what year did Berlin host the Olympic games?'); other times, they require deeper thinking (for example, 'Why was there growing demand for civil rights in America in 1945?'). Every teacher across the world uses targeted questions in virtually every lesson. However, most teachers' practice would probably be *even better* if they asked more of these. Do you think this applies to you?

Follow-up questions

A follow-up question is one that keeps the thinking going after a targeted question has been asked. There are two subtypes: **explorative** and **collaborative**.

- Explorative follow-up questions probe students' thinking or take it a step further. For example:
  - Why do you think that?
  - What makes you so sure about that?
  - Is there anything you do to help remember that?
  - Could you tell us a bit more about that?
- **Collaborative** follow-up questions encourage students to learn from each other. For example:
  - Do you agree?
  - Does anyone disagree?
  - Would anyone like to comment on that?
  - Who would like to say a bit more about that?
  - Could someone tell us why that is?

Specific input | Focused reflection | Deliberate practice

If you get into the habit of asking **at least one follow-up question** (explorative or collaborative) for every targeted question asked, suddenly, the total number of questions asked in a lesson at least doubles.

Pitfall Avoidance Principle

For every targeted question you ask, try to ask at least one follow-up question (explorative or collaborative).

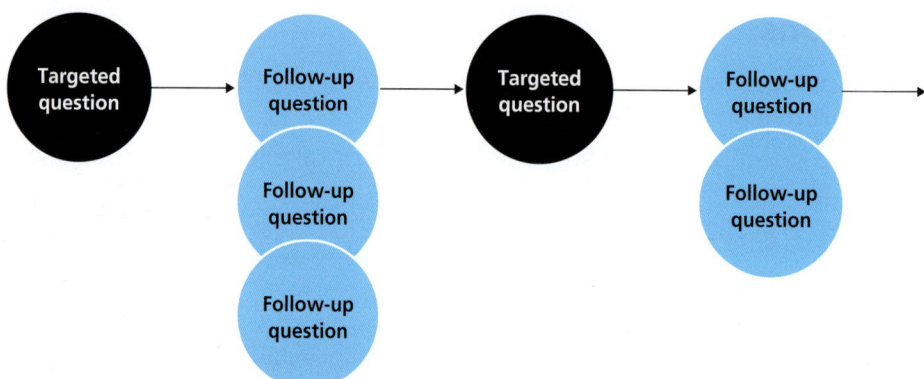

Common Pitfall 3: Talking for extended periods without asking a question

Regardless of how skilled we are at presenting, demonstrating, explaining or modelling, there is only so long we can talk before we should be asking a question. Leave it too long and we risk students' attention wandering or leaving students behind because they don't understand the things we are assuming they do. But how long is 'too long'? How often should we be asking students questions?

The answers to these questions are offered by our next Pitfall Avoidance Principle:

> **Pitfall Avoidance Principle**
>
> For every minute of teacher talk, try to ask at least one question.
>
>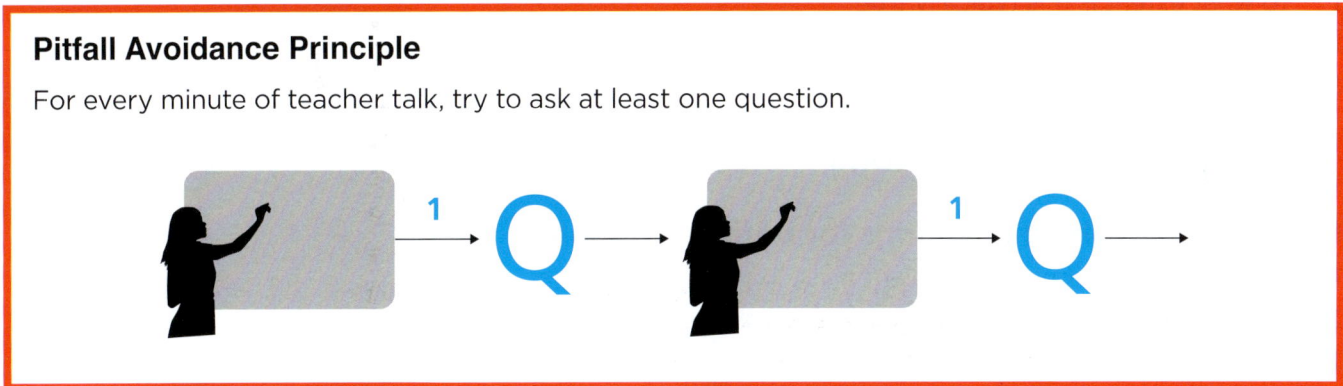

This principle *isn't* suggesting you set a phone alarm to go off once a minute in the teacher-led phase of a lesson. Rather, it is suggesting you get into the habit of making mental notes, or using lesson plans and teaching resources, to help you ask frequent questions. For example, including frequent preplanned questions in PowerPoint presentations can help. This is discussed further in the Trusted Technique **More Questions, More Often**.

Power-Up Prompts

Teacher exposition is infused with frequent questioning.
1. To what extent is this typically true?
2. What do you currently do to ensure this?
3. What could you do to make this *even better*?

Deeper-Thinking Questions

Reflection/coaching questions for before a lesson
1. How many questions do you plan to ask in this lesson?
2. Do you think you are planning to ask enough questions?
3. Thinking about the different phases of the lesson, is there scope to ask more questions in any particular phase?
4. What will you do to ensure you don't talk for too long without asking a question?
5. Is there anything you will do to keep track of the number of questions you ask or how long you go without asking a question?

Reflection/coaching questions for after a lesson
1. How many questions did you ask in this lesson?
2. Do you think you asked enough questions?
3. Thinking about the different phases of the lesson, was there scope to ask more questions in any particular phase?

4 Do you think you asked enough follow-up questions?

5 Were the follow-up questions you asked more *explorative* or *collaborative*?

6 Do you think there were any periods in the lesson where you talked for too long without asking a question?

7 What do you want to practise improving for future lessons?

Trusted Technique: More Questions, More Often

Rather than questions being asked sporadically, they are asked frequently; on average, at least once a minute.

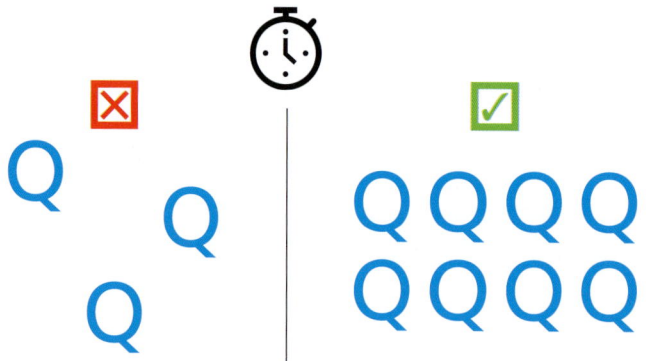

Why use it? (STAR: Spotlight, Thinking, Attention, Responding)

Asking **More Questions, More Often** creates more opportunities to find out what students know and understand.

This technique also creates more opportunities for students to think, helps to check and hold student attention, and creates more opportunities for you to explore students' thinking and learning.

Suggested steps

1   Use lesson planning time to map out when you plan to ask key targeted questions during the lesson. Build as many as you can into resources such as PowerPoint.

Specific input | Focused reflection | **Deliberate practice**

2. Whenever you ask a targeted question, ask at least one follow-up question (explorative or collaborative).

3. Try to keep a mental track of how long you are talking without asking a question. If more than a minute goes past, it's probably time to ask one (which may not be preplanned).

Example

In a maths lesson...

Teacher 'What is £2.70 to the nearest pound... Ruby?' [Targeted question.]

Ruby 'Um... £3.'

Teacher 'How sure are you?' [Explorative follow-up question.]

Ruby 'Not very sure.'

Teacher 'Okay, so can you tell us why you think the answer *might* be £3, please?' [Explorative follow-up question.]

Ruby 'Because the number after the decimal point is bigger than five.'

Teacher 'Okay, good. And what is the rule that we need to remember?' [Explorative follow-up question.]

Ruby 'That if the number after the decimal point is bigger than five, we should round up.'

Teacher 'Thanks, Ruby. Would anyone like to comment on what Ruby has said?' [Collaborative follow-up question.]

Several hands go up and the teacher picks a student to answer.

Specific input | Focused reflection | **Deliberate practice**

Max	'We also round up if the number after the decimal point *is* five – it's not just when it's bigger than five.'
Teacher	'That's an interesting point. What do you think… Hazel?' [Collaborative follow-up question.]
Hazel	'Yes. I think Max is right.'
Teacher	'And what do you think… Jodie?' [Collaborative follow-up question.]
Jodie	'Erm… I'm not sure.'
Teacher	'Jack – can you help?' [Collaborative follow-up question.]
Jack	'Yes. I think Max is right, too.'
Teacher	'Yes, Jack and Hazel. Max *is* right. So, Jodie, back to you. Can you tell us what the rule that we need to remember is, please?' [Collaborative follow-up question.]
Jodie	'We round up when the number after the decimal point is five or more than five.'
Teacher	'Well done, Jodie. That's very good. The rule we all need to remember is that we round up when the number after the decimal point is five or above. Let's all have a go at applying this rule to some different examples.'

Notes

The exchange in this example is likely to have lasted up to around two minutes. It involved *nine questions*, one of which was a targeted question and eight of which were follow-up questions. By using these, the teacher was able to get more students to think and to explore the thinking of more students. The learning became collaborative. If you contrast the approach taken with one in which the teacher had asked Ruby the targeted question and simply accepted her answer, the missed opportunities to widen and strengthen learning should be obvious.

Specific input | Focused reflection | **Deliberate practice**

Power up your questioning

Theme 2: Asking better questions
– *to encourage desirable thinking*

Overview

Common Pitfalls	Power-Up Prompts	Trusted Techniques
1. Asking 'throwaway questions'. 2. Focusing too much on surface knowledge at the expense of deeper understanding. 3. Misunderstanding the relationship between 'closed' and 'open' questions.	The questions you ask promote desirable thinking (which develops learning) as opposed to superficial thinking (which simply keeps students busy). Questioning is used to develop both surface knowledge and deeper understanding. ■ To what extent is this typically true? ■ What do you currently do to ensure this? ■ What could you do to make this *even better*?	Spotlight Assessment Activities Different Angles Difficulty Staircase

Common Pitfall 1: Asking 'throwaway questions'

We've all done it. In planning a lesson, we have considered the learning intention and the success criteria, and what we think are the best activities to achieve them. We have taken time to create a high-quality presentation for the teacher-led phase and to ensure there are high-quality resources for the supported practice phase that follows. However, what we haven't spent enough time doing is **planning the key targeted questions** that we want to ask students during the teacher-led phase.[46] Instead, we trust that we can rely on our subject knowledge and pedagogical skills to come up with good questions 'in the moment'. But pause and ask yourself: how good are you at doing that, really?

Some teachers are very good at this. Most aren't (though they often believe that they are). Being able to come up with questions in the moment isn't the same as being able to come up with *good* questions. Usually, good questions require good planning. Accepting this, the next logical question to ask ourselves is 'what is a "good" question, exactly?'

Desirable thinking: a Goldilocks principle

---

46 'Targeted questions' are discussed in Theme 1.

The most important criterion with which to judge the quality of a question is the extent to which it promotes **desirable thinking**.[47] Essentially, we are talking about a **Goldilocks principle**: not *too easy* and not *too difficult*. Ideally, teachers should always be aiming to ask questions that produce *at least some degree of cognitive struggle* while also giving students *a reasonable chance of success*.[48] Asking lots of questions pitched at the wrong difficulty level will do little to strengthen or advance learning. Question *frequency* (though important) and question *quality* are not the same thing.

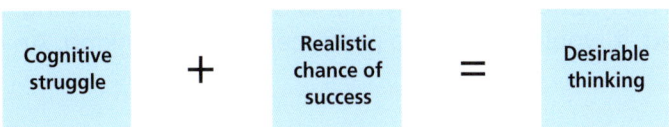

Throwaway questions

Throwaway questions are those that don't fit the Goldilocks principle. They tend to fall into one of three categories: too easy, too difficult or daft.

Too easy

The most common throwaway questions are those that are too easy. Students have a lot of success with them (which is a good thing), but these questions don't produce enough of a cognitive struggle to push learning forward or give teachers robust evidence of what students actually understand. For example, imagine you are teaching a class of 10-year-old students how to multiply by 10. You have explained how to do this and given several examples.

---

47 The term 'desirable thinking' is a variation on the concept of 'desirable difficulties', as discussed in Bjork, E.L. and Bjork, R.A. (2014) 'Making things hard on yourself, but in a good way.'

48 Full credit to Derek Huffman, principal teacher of pedagogy at Berwickshire High School, for framing this in this way.

To check understanding, you then ask students the following question:

What is 20 × 10?

A 200   **B** 550   **C** 600   **D** 1000.

To most students, it will be plainly obvious that options B, C and D are wrong. Almost no thought is required to dismiss them. This is a throwaway question because little cognitive struggle is required to answer it. It keeps students busy, but not in a way that is desirable for learning. If the question had been better planned and designed, it would likely have produced better thinking. An example of a better question might be:

What is 20 × 10?

A 2   **B** 200   **C** 220   **D** 2010.

Here, the distractors (incorrect answers) have been more carefully considered to be more plausible. They are competitive.[49] As a result, the thinking required to answer the question should be more desirable. The answers the teacher gets should also be more formatively valuable. For example, if they find out that 90% of the class chose option A, it's a good bet that 90% of the class have confused multiplication with division. This should help inform what the teacher does next.

The question could have been asked as the more straightforward 'what is 20 × 10?' (i.e. without multiple-choice options). However, the inclusion of options can be useful as a means to get students to think harder than they would have without them, and to tease out misconceptions that might have been left unchecked and uncorrected. So long as they are plausible, options can cause students to pause and think about things they might not have otherwise. For example, they might think to themselves silently: 'Hang on a minute, that *might* actually be right.'

---

[49] Bjork, E.L. and Bjork, R.A. (2014) 'Making things hard on yourself, but in a good way.'

Too difficult

Questions that are too difficult for students to answer are also throwaway questions. True, they produce cognitive struggle, but because they don't give students a realistic chance of success, the difficulty they pose isn't a desirable one. Questions that are too difficult tend to be the result of students either lacking sufficient background knowledge or having to think about too much at one time.

However, on balance, questions that are too difficult are usually less of an issue in lessons than questions that are too easy because difficult questions can be made easier. For example, a question that is proving too difficult for a student to answer can be broken down into a set of simpler questions which, in the end, support the student to arrive at the correct answer to the original question.[50]

Daft

The final category of throwaway question is those that are simply daft.[51] These are the sorts of questions that lead students to think, 'What?', 'I've no idea' or *Obviously…*' For example:

- In a maths lesson: 'What do you think is a safe amount of money to carry in your wallet?'
- In a geography lesson: 'Would you rather live in Singapore or Slovakia?'[52]
- In a modern studies lesson: 'Do you think discrimination is a bad thing?'
- In a science lesson: 'Do you think it's a good idea to touch the red-hot metal?'

Almost always, daft questions are the result of poor lesson planning. At best, asking them wastes time. At worst, doing so can have a negative effect on learning because they frustrate or confuse students.

---

50 We will explore this further in Theme 6.
51 Yes, there *can* be such a thing as a daft question.
52 We are assuming here that the class hasn't been taught anything about either of these countries.

Specific input | Focused reflection | Deliberate practice

Pitfall Avoidance Principle

Plan and ask questions with 'desirable thinking' in mind. Avoid questions that could be classed as 'throwaway'.

❌ Questions that require no struggle to answer

❌ Questions that offer no chance of success

❌ Questions that could be classified as daft

✅ Questions that require a **degree of struggle** and offer a **fair chance of success**

Common Pitfall 2: Focusing too much on surface knowledge at the expense of deeper understanding

Should lessons focus on 'higher-order' thinking?

When school leaders and inspectors observe lessons, it isn't uncommon for them to tell teachers things like 'There weren't enough higher-order questions' or 'The lesson didn't focus enough on higher-order thinking'. However, I would argue that such statements aren't particularly helpful because there is too much ambiguity as to what they actually mean.[53] I *think* what these people are trying to get at is that

---

[53] I'm going to suggest that this is also ambiguous in the minds of the school leaders and inspectors who make these comments. Push them to give specific examples and watch them get stumped.

they want teachers to be asking more questions that relate to the upper sections of Bloom's taxonomy pyramid:

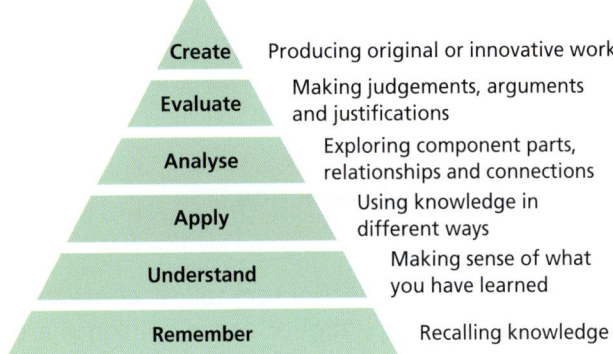

However, there are several issues with this, which we will explore here.

The first issue is that Benjamin Bloom did not represent his original taxonomy in this way. The pyramid representation has been subsequently created by others.[54] Bloom wasn't trying to suggest that there is a hierarchy of thinking skills as the pyramid illustrates. Rather, he was making the point that **knowledge is the bedrock of thinking**. This is why Dylan Wiliam has suggested that a better representation of the taxonomy would be as follows:[55]

---

54 Hendrick, C. and Macpherson, R. (2017) *What Does This Look Like in the Classroom?*
55 https://x.com/dylanwiliam/status/849277989577789441?lang=en-GB

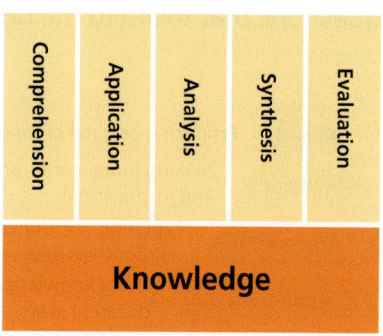

The second issue arises when school leaders and inspectors tell teachers that the upper sections of the pyramid ('create', 'evaluate', 'analyse' and 'apply' – 'higher-order' thinking) are more important than the lower ones ('remember' and 'understand'), when the reality is that *both* are important. The ability to create, evaluate, analyse and apply is *dependent* on the knowledge and understanding students have.[56]

The third issue arises when school leaders and inspectors expect to see 'higher-order' thinking in every lesson they observe. That's not a realistic expectation because, a lot of the time, teachers will be working with students to develop knowledge and understanding (the lower regions of the pyramid). That doesn't mean that students shouldn't be *thinking* – they absolutely should – but it does mean this won't necessarily be creative, evaluative or analytical in nature.

---

56 Hirsch, E.D. (2016) *Why Knowledge Matters*.

Flipping the pyramid: surface knowledge and deeper understanding

As a means to avoiding all these issues, rather than talk about 'lower-order' and 'higher-order' thinking, I would argue that it is better to refer to '**surface knowledge**' and '**deeper understanding**' with a 'flipped pyramid' in mind:

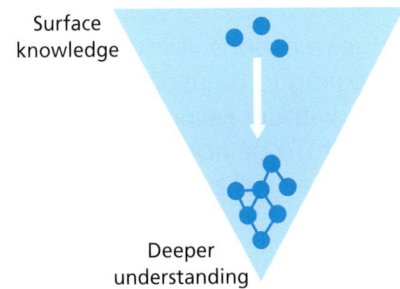

The flipped pyramid shows the development of surface knowledge as a necessary first step to deeper understanding. It makes clear that *both* are important and interrelated – it's not about one or the other. The more surface knowledge students acquire, and the more connections get made, the more they are likely to understand something. Teachers should be using a combination of surface knowledge questions and deeper understanding questions to develop both the top and bottom areas of the pyramid.

Surface knowledge questions

Surface knowledge questions principally relate to *recall*. For example:
- What type of shape is this?
- Which element has the symbol Br?
- Which part of the brain controls balance?

Specific input | Focused reflection | Deliberate practice

It is important teachers use questions like this to both **check** students have specific surface knowledge and **strengthen** this (remember the testing effect that was discussed earlier in this book – *retrieval strengthens memory*).

Deeper understanding questions

However, if we only ask surface knowledge questions, it is unlikely students will develop the deeper understanding that is so important for learning to be useful. We aren't aiming for students to be able to recite facts and concepts in parrot-fashion without being able to *do* anything with these. The ability to use knowledge is the main reason for teaching it. To be able to do this, students need to *understand* things. The more they understand, the more likely they will be able to apply knowledge accurately in a variety of situations, including those that are unfamiliar.

For example, students might have learned that the definition of a molecule is 'a group of atoms covalently bonded together'. This is surface knowledge. They might have also learned some common examples of molecules, including H_2, O_2 and CO_2. This is also surface knowledge. If you ask them 'What is the definition of a molecule?' or 'Can you give two examples of molecules?', the surface knowledge they have learned means students can probably do both. However, it is less certain that they will be able to answer **deeper understanding questions** that require the *application of knowledge*, such as these:

- Which of the following is *not* a molecule? HCl, H_2SO_4, FeO
- Why is HCl a molecule but $MgCl_2$ isn't?
- True or false: Fe_2O_3 is a molecule (and explain why).

Each of these questions requires students to apply knowledge in ways that have never been asked to before. In doing so, they both check and develop deeper understanding.

The more we understand, the less likely we are to forget

In addition to its role in helping students to apply knowledge, the development of understanding plays a key role in preventing forgetting. To appreciate this, think of surface knowledge as being like a balloon, with deeper understanding being the tether that stops this floating away:

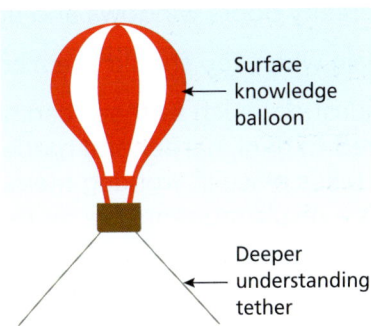

The more students understand, the stronger the tether and the less likely they are to forget.

How do we develop deeper understanding?

The key to developing students' deeper understanding is to get them to think **hard about content in a variety of ways**. The Trusted Techniques **Spotlight Assessment Activities** and **Different Angles** can help with this.

For example, in an English lesson students might have developed surface knowledge about what commas are and been shown examples of when to use them. The following questions are targeted ones, designed to develop deeper understanding:

Question 1: Find the deliberate mistakes in the following sentence:

Last week, we all went to Disneyland Paris, which everyone enjoyed very very much.

Question 2: In which part(s) of the following sentence should you put a comma?

It was a spooky spooky house with creeky doors windows and floorboards.

Question 3: In your own words, explain when you should use a comma in a sentence.[57]

Through careful planning and design, questions such as these can be sequenced as a **Difficulty Staircase**, whereby students are required to think harder and harder with each passing question. The harder they think, the more processing takes place in working memory, and the more connections get made within and between schemata. As a result, students are more likely to understand and less likely to forget.

Pitfall Avoidance Principle

Focus on ensuring there is a blend of both surface knowledge (recall) and deeper understanding (application) questions when planning and delivering lessons.

---

57 This is an example of 'generative learning'. Generative learning involves knowledge retrieval but goes beyond this, for example, by asking students to put something in their own words or to represent a concept as a picture.

Common Pitfall 3: Misunderstanding the relationship between 'closed' and 'open' questions

True or false:

1. It is more important for students to answer open questions than closed ones.
2. Open questions are better for probing understanding and getting students to think hard than closed questions.

Many teachers and school leaders believe the answer to both of these questions is true. However, they are actually both false. Let's explore this.

What are closed and open questions?

'Closed questions' are those that have a specific correct answer; 'open questions' are those that don't. For example:

Closed questions	Open questions

■ True or false: the Earth orbits the sun.
■ How many days does it take for the Earth to orbit the sun?
■ How many hours does it take for the Earth to orbit the sun?
■ In which month does the northern hemisphere receive sunlight for the longest period?
■ Why does the northern hemisphere receive more sunlight in June than December?
	■ What do you know about how the Earth orbits the sun?
	■ What do you see in this diagram of the solar system?
	■ In terms of the Earth orbiting the sun, which month would you say is the odd one out, and why?
	  a January
	  b June
	  c September.
	■ What are your main takeaway points from our discussion of the Earth orbiting the sun in the last 15 minutes?

Specific input | Focused reflection | Deliberate practice

Common misunderstandings

Most teachers and school leaders appreciate the distinction between closed and open questions. However, many misunderstand the role that each can play when it comes to students' thinking and learning. The most common misunderstanding is that open questions are better for getting students to think harder and for teachers to probe deeper understanding. This is probably the reason why so many teachers are told to 'ask more open questions' (and fewer closed ones) in lesson observation feedback. However, this isn't necessarily great advice.

It's true that open questions *can* be good for getting students to think hard and to probe deeper understanding. However, they won't always do that. For example, if you ask, 'What do you know about how the Earth orbits the sun?', students might reel off a series of surface knowledge facts (which are useful for you to know *they* know) but offer no evidence of any deeper understanding. At their worst, they can be 'daft questions' (as previously discussed), such as 'What do you think is a safe amount of money to carry in your wallet?'.

Also, closed questions can be just as effective – if not more effective – at getting students to think hard and probe deeper understanding.[58] For example, if you ask, 'Why does the northern hemisphere receive more sunlight in June than December?', a lot of thinking is required to answer that.

The key point for teachers and school leaders to appreciate is that open and closed questions *both* have important roles to play in the teaching and learning process. Both can target surface knowledge, and both can target deeper understanding. One type is not necessarily better than the other. **The best type to use depends on what the teacher is trying to do**.

---

58 Barton, C. (2018) *How I Wish I'd Taught Maths*.

The right type for the right purpose

If you are trying to find out as much as possible about what students know and understand (which could be at any point during a lesson), then it's probably best to use open questions. If you want students to think about specific things or find out specific things students know and understand, then it's probably best to use closed questions.

When teaching is at its best, there is likely to be a blend of both open and closed questions, all of which have been well planned or carefully considered. The proportion of each type is far less important than the extent to which the teacher's aims are achieved by asking *good* questions.

Pitfall Avoidance Principle

Plan for a blend of both closed and open questions (and don't get too hung up if there is more of one than the other). Don't ask more open questions just because you think that's what you're meant to do.

Power-Up Prompts

The questions you ask promote desirable thinking (which develops learning) as opposed to superficial thinking (which simply keeps students busy).

Questioning is used to develop both surface knowledge and deeper understanding.

1. To what extent is this typically true?
2. What do you currently do to ensure this?
3. What could you do to make this *even better*?

Deeper-Thinking Questions

Reflection/coaching questions for *before* a lesson

1. Are there particular questions you think you should ask to explore students' prior knowledge (relating to this lesson)?
2. Are there particular questions you think you should ask to explore students' understanding during teaching?
3. Could any of the questions you have planned be classified as 'throwaway'?
4. What steps do you plan to take in this lesson to ensure questions are developing and checking deeper understanding (alongside surface knowledge)?
5. Are there any particular Trusted Techniques you will be focusing on?
6. If so, what are the specific aspects of these techniques you will consciously try to do well?

Reflection/coaching questions for *after* a lesson

1. How many questions had you planned for this lesson?
2. How well did you use questioning to explore students' prior knowledge (relating to this lesson)?
3. How well did you use questioning to explore students' deeper understanding during teaching?
4. How effectively did you use **Spotlight Assessment Activities** in this lesson?
5. Was there scope to use more Spotlight Assessments? If so, in which part(s) of the lesson could you have done this?
6. How effectively did you use the information you got from Spotlight Assessments in a formative sense (that is, to adjust your teaching and give feedback to students)?

7   To what extent did you use questioning to explore students' thinking from **Different Angles**?
8   Do you think you made effective use of a **Difficulty Staircase** approach to questioning? Is there anything you could have done to make this even better?

Trusted Technique 1: Spotlight Assessment Activities

Spotlight Assessment Activities are questions and tasks that help students to think hard about specific things in a carefully curated way. Usually they focus on bringing common misconceptions to the surface. Examples include True or False, Odd One Out, Deliberate Mistakes, Concept Cartoons, Multiple Choice, Compare and Contrast, Tell Me Why and Empty Your Brain.

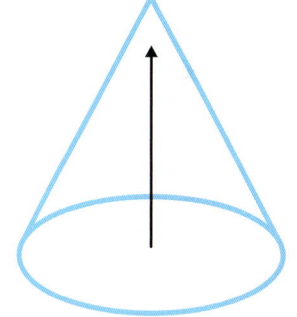

Why use it? (STAR: Spotlight, Thinking, Attention, Responding)

Spotlight Assessment Activities encourage students to think about things in ways that more straightforward recall questions might not. As a result, they can help students develop knowledge connections, leading to deeper understanding and strengthened memory. By 'shining a spotlight' on specific things that students know and understand (or don't), they produce powerful formative information to which you can respond. Beyond this, they bring variety to the sorts of questions you are asking, which can make lessons more interesting.

Suggested steps

1 Choose a section of content you want students to think about and that you want to check understanding of.
2 Individually or with a colleague, brainstorm common mistakes and misconceptions relating to this. These might have come from real answers you have been given when teaching something previously.
3 With the principle of desirable thinking in mind, design a Spotlight Assessment Activity that encourages students to think about this content (for example, True or False, Deliberate Mistakes or Multiple Choice).

Examples

True or False	0.066 is the same as 66%. Green is a primary colour. When nails get rusty, they get heavier. Two of the angles in an isosceles triangle will always be the same size.
Odd One Out	7, 9, 11, 13 Spider, Shark, Swallow, Snake Accelerando, Adagio, Allegro, Moderato
Deliberate Mistakes	To calculate the circumference of a circle with a diameter of 20cm, the calculation would be: 2 × 3.14 × 20. To find out how far east or west a place is, lines of latitude are used. These lines run parallel to the equator. The chemical symbol for gold is Ag.

Specific input | Focused reflection | **Deliberate practice**

Concept Cartoons[59]

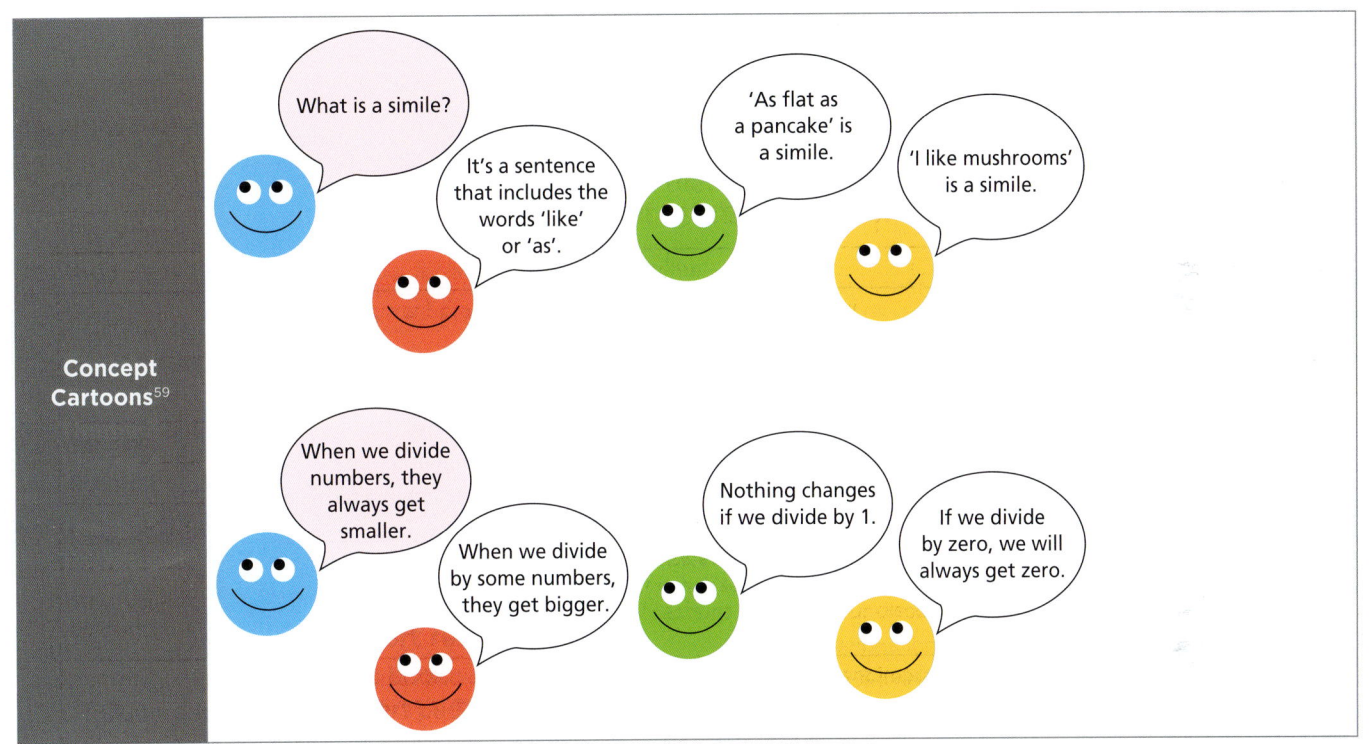

---

59 Adapted from Naylor, S., Keogh, B. and Goldsworthy, A. (2004) *Active Assessment: Thinking, Learning and Assessment in Science*.

Multiple Choice	Which fraction is the largest? A 1/2 B 3/4 C 1/10 Which of the following statements about acids is true: A The higher the pH of a chemical, the more acidic it is. B Adding water to an acid increases the pH. C A chemical with a pH of 9 is an acid. Liberal ideology...[60] A Was invented in the 18th century to serve the interests of the British Liberal Party. B Developed as a hostile response to the emergence of industrial capitalism. C Is a compromise between socialism and conservatism. D Is a long-established creed that focuses on individual freedom.
Compare and Contrast	What are the similarities and differences between Macbeth and Lady Macbeth? What do hormones have in common with enzymes, and what makes them different? What does the formula for the circumference of a circle have in common with the formula for the area of a circle, and what differences are there between them?
Tell Me Why	Why is 19 a prime number? Why does the sun rise in the east? Why is 'I like potatoes' not a simile? Why is a frog an amphibian but a snake is a reptile?
Empty Your Brain	Write down everything you know about the rules of basketball. Tell a partner everything you know about safety rules for the workshop.

---

60 Christodoulou, D. (2016) *Making Good Progress?*

Notes

Spotlight Assessment Activities can add value to all stages of a lesson – beginning, middle and end. For example, they can be used at the start to explore students' prior knowledge; they can be used during the course of a lesson to check understanding or to get students to think about particular things in different ways; or they can be used towards the end of a lesson to check knowledge and understanding (short-term learning).

To be most effective, Spotlight Assessment Activities usually need to be preplanned. Working with colleagues to design these can be an incredibly valuable professional learning experience. They do take time and effort to create but, once you have them, you have them forever.

As with all questions, we are trying to promote desirable thinking. Questions that are too easy (or difficult) won't achieve that. For example, if you are teaching an English literature lesson about *Macbeth* to a class of 15-year-olds and you ask, 'True or False: Macbeth was Scottish,' you have got students to think, but not in a desirably difficult way. A better question might be: 'True or False: Banquo discovers Duncan's body.'

In Spotlight Assessment Activities that offer a choice of answers (such as Deliberate Mistakes and Multiple Choice), not telling students how many correct answers there are should get them to *think harder,* making the question more desirably difficult.

Also, in questions with a choice, try to **avoid 'throwaway' distractors**. Every incorrect option should require at least *some* consideration. An example of a question with throwaway distractors to a class of 16-year-olds who have been learning about DNA might be:

Which of the following does DNA stand for?

A Destabilising nuclear activity

B Deoxyribonucleic acid

C Dynamite not allowed

D Doughnuts never available.[61]

To avoid students guessing or arriving at correct answers via a misconception, always try to follow up on students' answers by asking them to explain their thinking. For example, with True or False, if a student says 'false', ask them:

- 'Why is it false?'
- 'What would make it true?'

There is often a great deal of value in combining **Spotlight Assessment Activities** with other Trusted Techniques, such as **Show-Me Boards** and/or **Chat to a Partner**.

Trusted Technique 2: Different Angles

A series of related questions is used to get students to think about the same content but in different ways. The questions might be used over the course of a single lesson, across multiple lessons or in homework.

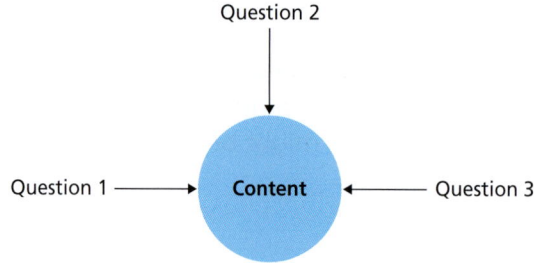

---

61 You might be surprised how commonly questions with throwaway distractors like this appear in lessons.

Why use it? (STAR: Spotlight, Thinking, Attention, Responding)

By thinking about the same content in different ways, students develop knowledge connections that both deepen understanding and strengthen memory. This makes it more likely that students will be able to apply their knowledge correctly in future and less likely that knowledge will be forgotten.

Asking students multiple questions about the same content should get them to think harder than they would have if only one question was asked. If a period of time is allowed to pass between each question (which might be minutes, days or weeks) the forgetting effect can be utilised to further strengthen memory.[62]

Suggested steps

1   Choose a topic or concept you want students to think about.
2   Individually or with a colleague, brainstorm different questions that could be used to get students to think about this in different ways. This might include using **Spotlight Assessment Activities**.
3   Plan the most appropriate points in a lesson or series of lessons to ask each of these questions. Alternatively, include them in homework.

Example

Across a series of science lessons...

Angle 1: Having been taught about filtration earlier in the lesson, students are asked to label the following diagram:

---

[62] The forgetting effect was discussed in the 'Learning and how it happens' section.

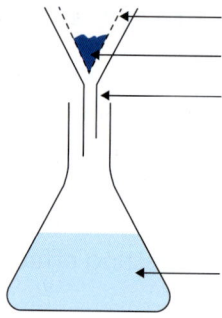

Angle 2 (in the same lesson): In their own words, students are asked to describe what is going on in the diagram.

Angle 3 (in the next lesson): Students are asked a series of True or False questions about filtration, such as:

- True or False: The substance left behind in the filter paper is called the filtrate.
- True or False: If a mixture of salt, sand and water was filtered, only the sand would be left in the filter paper.

Where an answer is false, students are asked to correct it.

Angle 4 (in a homework exercise): Students are shown a filtration diagram that includes deliberate mistakes. They are asked to identify all of these and to correct them.

Notes

Sometimes, all you need to do to change the angle of a question is to reverse what it is asking. For example:

Specific input | Focused reflection | **Deliberate practice**

Angle 1: What is the chemical formula for methane? (The answer is CH_4.)

Angle 2: What is the name of the chemical with the formula CH_4? (The answer is methane.)

Clearly, you wouldn't ask the Angle 1 and 2 questions in immediate succession. That wouldn't create a desirable difficulty. Rather, you would allow some time to pass before asking the different version. How much would be a matter of professional judgement.

Trusted Technique 3: Difficulty Staircase

You ask a sequence of questions about the same content that get progressively more challenging.

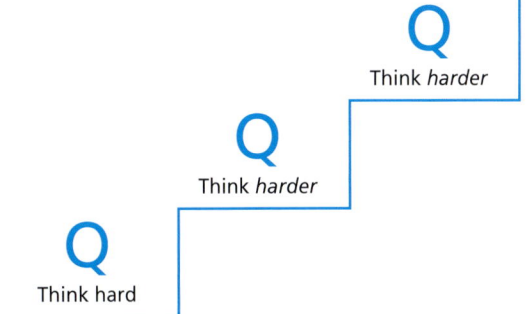

Why use it? (STAR: Spotlight, Thinking, Attention, Responding)

Asking students multiple questions about the same content should get them to think about this more than they would have if only one question was asked. As questions get more challenging, students will be required to think harder. This will help develop knowledge connections and strengthen memory.

The more questions you ask, the more detail you get about the depth of students' understanding. The success of answering questions that get progressively more challenging should be motivating to students, producing a sense of accomplishment and keeping them interested.

Suggested steps

1. You ask a question.
2. You get evidence that *at least 80% of the class* can answer this correctly (for example, you might use **Show-Me Boards**), giving feedback as appropriate. If you haven't reached at least 80% success, you do some reteaching and either ask the question again or ask one that is very similar.
3. With 80% success achieved, you ask another question about the same content that is incrementally more challenging than the original.
4. Repeat steps 1–3 at least once.

Example

In a science lesson, having taught a class of 13-year-old students the basics of series circuits, you share the following diagram and ask a sequence of **Difficulty Staircase** *questions:*

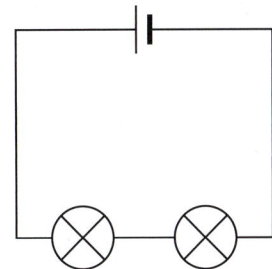

Stair 1: How many different components are in this circuit?

Stair 2: What are the names of these components? [More challenging.]

Stair 3: What is the function of the cell? [More challenging.]

Stair 4: What would happen to the brightness of the bulbs if the length of the wires was increased? [More challenging.]

Stair 5: Suggest one change to the circuit that would make the brightness of the bulbs dimmer. [More challenging.]

Notes

The 80% Success Rule[63] doesn't mean you ignore the 20% of students who can't answer or have answered incorrectly. By giving feedback on each stair, you should be addressing some of the issues these students had. For the small number of students who continue to struggle despite this feedback, you

---

63 Discussed in more detail as part of Theme 6.

should make time later in the lesson to do some one-to-one or small-group teaching while others in the class work on consolidation or extension material.

Be careful not to increase the level of challenge too far, too quickly. If the steps are too big, students won't be able to climb them. Also, don't be afraid to 'ham up' the difficulty a question poses. For example, you might say, 'The next question is a *really* challenging one. I'm going to be so impressed if everyone can get this one right!' This should increase students' sense of accomplishment.

Because it can be difficult to 'plan a staircase' in the moment, it is usually best to plan **Difficulty Staircase** questions in advance of a lesson, individually or – even better – with a colleague.

Power up your questioning

Theme 3: Getting more students to think about each question
– so more students are learning

Overview

Common Pitfalls	Power-Up Prompts	Trusted Techniques
1. Allowing shouting out. 2. A lack of thinking time. 3. Creating 'thinking get-outs'.	*Every student* is expected to think about *every question* asked. ■ To what extent is this typically true? ■ What do you currently do to ensure this? ■ What could you do to make this *even better*?	Pause Show-Me Boards Chat to a Partner Patient Hands Cold Call On the Hook Choral Response

Common Pitfall 1: Allowing shouting out

Of all the things that should probably *never* happen in a lesson, students shouting out answers to questions is a good contender to be at the top of any list.[64]

Why is shouting out such an issue?

Shouting out is the enemy of whole-class thinking. If you allow a student to shout out, you are effectively signalling to the class that it doesn't matter who thinks about this question – 'I just need an answer from *someone*.'

But of course, that's not what we want. We're not interested in the thinking and learning of the class as an *entity* – we're interested in the thinking and learning of every *individual* in the class. **Our responsibility is to support and challenge everyone to learn all of the content we have set out in our curriculum** (however aspirational that might be). No student has the right to stop others from learning this, which means no student has the right to deny anyone the opportunity to think about any question we ask.

With very few exceptions, every student should be expected to think about every question we ask. To ensure this happens, we need to make sure students are clear about this expectation, and we need to teach them to behave in a way that supports this.

What should I do if a student shouts out?

As tempting as it might be to accept an answer that is shouted out, you should never do this. Your acceptance rewards unacceptable behaviour and makes it more likely this will happen again. Instead, you should do one of two things:

---

[64] As with any rule, there might be the odd occasion when you decide it can be broken. However, the important point is that it is you who decides, not the students.

Specific input | Focused reflection | Deliberate practice

1. **Ignore what was said and choose a different student to answer**. The fact that you have ignored the shouted-out answer should make it clear that this shouldn't have happened.
2. **Ignore what was said, reprimand and/or remind the student of the rule, then choose a different student to answer**. For example, you might say: 'We don't shout out in this class, Johnnie. Everyone needs the opportunity to think about the questions I ask. Make sure you give them the opportunity to do that next time. Thanks.'

It is arguable which approach is better. For example, though they can often be important, reprimands and reminders can disrupt the flow of the lesson. Ideally, teachers should be aiming to create a culture in which neither is needed because students have learned never to shout out.

Pitfall Avoidance Principle

Don't tolerate shouting out.

 Question → Answer shouted out → Accept (even with a reprimand/reminder)

 Question → Answer shouted out → **Ignore → Ask another student**

 Question → Answer shouted out → **Ignore and reprimand/remind → Ask another student**

Common Pitfall 2: A lack of thinking time

Because a key purpose of questioning is to get students to think, it is important we give students sufficient time to do this using techniques such as **Pause**. However, many teachers don't. Instead, they ask questions expecting to get immediate answers. Sometimes, when they don't get an answer quickly,

Specific input | Focused reflection | Deliberate practice

teachers ask another student, even though the first student could have answered if they'd been given a few seconds longer.

Questioning doesn't need to be rapid-fire, and quickness of response isn't usually something to get too hung up about. The most important principle is that students are given sufficient **thinking time** whenever you ask a question.

How much thinking time should I give?

How much thinking time you give is a matter of professional judgement. It will depend on factors including the difficulty or complexity of the question and the confidence of the student. For most questions, three to five seconds is probably enough. However, don't be afraid to offer more if you think that would be beneficial.

Trusted Techniques such as **Show-Me Boards** and **Chat to a Partner** automatically build thinking time into them and are worth making an integral feature of your regular teaching if you are aiming to get better at giving enough thinking time.

Pitfall Avoidance Principle

Always allow at least a few seconds of thinking time after asking a question.

 Question → Answer → Question → Answer …

 Question → **Wait** → Answer → Question → **Wait** → Answer …

Common Pitfall 3: Creating 'thinking get-outs'

In *Teach Like a Champion 3.0*, Doug Lemov offers a useful diagram to summarise what we should be aiming for with our questioning:[65]

The 'sweet spot', in which **all students are thinking in a desirably difficult way**, is highlighted in red. This is the area we should always be aiming to hit. Even if it isn't possible to get every student to answer every question aloud, every student should be thinking about every question, and every question should pose at least some form of desirable difficulty.[66]

---

65 The version presented here is an adaptation of that presented in *Teach Like a Champion 3.0* (which doesn't highlight the red 'sweet spot').

66 Naturally, some questions *will* be more straightforward to answer than others, but that isn't necessarily a bad thing. For example, students' experience of success with 'easier' questions can help develop their confidence and willingness to attempt more difficult ones later on.

However, hitting this sweet spot every time is one of the great challenges in teaching. Why do you think that is? Often, it is because many students aren't thinking about the questions we are asking them (even though we may believe that they are). What can we do about that?

How can we encourage every student to think about every question asked?

One of the things we can do to encourage all students to think about every question asked is ensure we allow at least *some* thinking time whenever we ask a question using techniques such as **Pause**. Other things relate to how we choose which students to answer.

Ignoring hands

When teachers ask a question and students' hands go up, it can be tempting to do one of two things:

1   Choose a student who is *quick to put up their hand*.
2   Choose *only students who put up their hand.*

However, if we do either of these things, we create a **thinking get-out** for everyone else. Students learn that if they don't put up their hand, they won't be asked to answer, which means they don't have to think. This is not okay. If everyone's learning is equally important, we can't allow some students to participate actively while others remain passive. **All students need to be active in their participation**. The most confident and enthusiastic can't be allowed to dominate, just as those who are less confident can't be allowed to 'opt out'. If we let either of these things happen, we will only accelerate the development of learning gaps between students. Being quick to put up your hand should not be a guarantee of being asked to answer. Not putting up your hand shouldn't be a guarantee you won't be asked.

In cases where students put up their hand quickly to answer, you can use the technique **Patient Hands**. With this, you can smile or nod in recognition of students' enthusiasm, but you should also wait at least a few seconds to convey your expectation that *everyone* should be thinking about your question. You might say things like:

- 'I'd like to see a few more hands, please.'
- 'I can see a few hands up, but I'd like *everyone* to be thinking about this. I'm going to wait for a few more.'
- 'Thanks to those who have put their hands up. I'm going to wait a few seconds longer and then I'm going to choose someone to answer.'

Or you might say nothing and simply wait, embracing the silence.

Even if a student hasn't put up their hand up to answer, you can still ask them to, saying things like:

- 'I know you haven't put your hand up, but I'd like to know what you think, please… Susan.'
- 'I'm really interested in what you have to say about this. Would you mind having a go please… Sharon?'

This is **Cold Call**.[67]

To be clear: you aren't using Cold Call to be unkind – quite the opposite. In as supportive a way as possible, you are using the technique to try to push everyone to think and participate, so you can respond appropriately and help everyone's learning.[68] Cold Call helps to convey that every student's voice matters and you want to hear from everyone. It supports 'voice equity'.[69] This includes those who might lack confidence and those who, if we're being honest, are just being lazy.

---

67 Lemov, D. (2015) *Teach Like a Champion 3.0*.
68 With this in mind, perhaps the technique should be rebranded '**Cold Call – Warmly**'.
69 Ibid.

Pitfall Avoidance Principle

Don't immediately choose the first (or second or third) student who puts up their hand to answer a question – wait a little longer for other hands to go up or choose someone who doesn't have their hand up.

 Question → Hands up → A quick volunteer

 Question → Hands up → **Wait for more hands** → **Ask a student with their hand up**

 Question → Hands up → **Wait** → **Ask a student without their hand up**

Random name generators vs mental notes

Some teachers use 'random name generators' such as lollipop sticks to encourage all students to think about questions. For example, whenever a question is asked, a lollipop stick is pulled from a jar and whoever's name is written on it is asked to answer.

If this is an approach you find useful, then great. However, I'd encourage you to keep two points in mind when using it:

1. You should always put sticks back into the jar after an answer is given so students know they could be chosen again. Otherwise, we create a thinking get-out.

2. Not knowing whose name will come out of the jar can remove the teacher's freedom to target particular questions at particular students. In other words, it can remove a potentially valuable

opportunity for differentiation.[70] For example, perhaps a particular student struggled with a particular question in the last lesson and the teacher wants to know whether they can answer it now. Or perhaps the teacher wants to ask a particular student a relatively straightforward question to build their confidence and willingness to participate.

Rather than using random name generators, I think it is better for teachers to make mental or written notes (perhaps using a tally chart on a seating plan) to keep track of who has answered questions. For me, this preserves the scope for professional decision making. Regardless, the most important point to keep in mind is that no matter how we are choosing students to answer, we should be doing as much as we can to encourage **all students to think** and to **avoid thinking get-outs**. **On the Hook** and **Choral Response** are other Trusted Techniques that can help.

---

70 By 'differentiation', we mean targeted support and challenge.

Power-Up Prompts

Every student is expected to think about *every question* asked.
1. To what extent is this typically true?
2. What do you currently do to ensure this?
3. What could you do to make this *even better*?

Deeper-Thinking Questions

Reflection/coaching questions for *before* a lesson:
1. What steps do you plan to take in this lesson to get *all students* to think about *every question* you ask?
2. Are there particular Trusted Techniques you will be focusing on?
3. If so, what specific aspects of these techniques will you consciously be trying to do well?

Reflection/coaching questions for *after* a lesson:
1. To what extent do you feel every student was given the opportunity to think about every question asked?
2. What, if anything, could you have done to give more students the opportunity to think about every question?
3. Were there particular Trusted Techniques you were using to get more students to think about your questions?
4. How successful do you think these were?
5. Is there anything you think you could have done to make these more successful?
6. Are there any other techniques you could use to make this even better?

Specific input | **Focused reflection** | Deliberate practice

Trusted Technique 1: Pause

You ask a question and allow at least a few seconds' thinking time before asking anyone to answer.

Why use it? (STAR: Spotlight, Thinking, Attention, Responding)

Pausing should encourage more students to think. It should also address 'rabbit in the headlight' moments whereby a student panics and tells you 'I don't know' (even though they do) because they didn't have enough time to think.

Suggested steps

1. You ask a question and follow up with a phrase such as:
   - 'Everyone think about that.'
   - 'Take a moment to think about that, everyone.'
   - '10 seconds' thinking time.'

   Alternatively, you say nothing and wait.

2. As you wait, scan the room and use your body language to convey an expectation that everyone should be thinking. Ignore any hands that go up. If you need to, count the amount of thinking time you said you would give in your head.

Specific input | Focused reflection | **Deliberate practice**

3 Choose a student to answer.

Example

In a German language lesson...

Teacher   'How do we ask where the nearest train station is? Ten seconds to think about that, everyone.'

Ten seconds pass, which the teacher counts in their head.

Teacher   'Okay, tell us what you think, please... Stephanie.'

Notes

The amount of thinking time you allow will depend on the difficulty or complexity of the question you ask. Sometimes, all that will be needed is a few seconds. Other times, it might be a minute or more. Use your judgement.

Try not to fall into the trap of saying anything during thinking time. Instead, **embrace the silence**. Students can't think *and* listen to what you're saying. Similarly, don't give in to any temptation to choose 'keen students' to answer before the thinking time is over, even if they put their hand up or gesture vociferously for your attention.

If you have established a 'thinking-time culture', you might not need to say things like 'everyone think about that'. Instead, everyone just *knows* this is the expectation. That said, it probably doesn't hurt to give reminders from time to time.

Trusted Technique 2: Show-Me Boards

You ask a question to which all students are expected to write (or draw) a response on mini-whiteboards, holding these up for you to see when told.

Why use it? (STAR: Spotlight, Thinking, Attention, Responding)

Show-Me Boards encourage all students to think and give everyone time to think. They encourage active participation from everyone and require all students to commit to a specific answer.

Most valuably, Show-Me Boards make the thinking or learning of all students visible so you can respond (either in the moment or at some point in the future).

Suggested steps

1 You ask a question and tell students to write (or draw) answers on Show-Me Boards, making it clear whether they should hold these up when they are ready or whether they are to wait until you tell everyone to hold boards up together.

2 [Optional.] You circulate the room having a look at what is being written on boards and give bits of feedback if appropriate.

Specific input | Focused reflection | **Deliberate practice**

3   If students have been told to hold boards up together, you give a signal for that to happen. Otherwise, you start to look at boards as they are being held up (and perhaps give a reminder for students to hold up boards when ready).

4   You look at the boards and take in as much information as possible. As you do this, you might make comments towards individual boards, such as 'Good', 'I like that', 'Nearly' or 'You've just made one small mistake – have another look at that.'

5   You address the class and either summarise what you have seen or ask students to share what they have written. You might also ask them to explain their answers.

Example

In a maths lesson...

Teacher 'On Show-Me Boards, I'd like to see the first five multiples of four. Hold your board up when you are ready.'

The teacher scans the room and waits for boards to start to go up. As they do this, they make comments to individuals.

Teacher [To student A.] 'That's perfect.' [To student B.] 'Nearly – but you've missed one out. Keep thinking.' [To student C.] 'No, those are multiples of two. Have another go.'

Teacher [To the class.] 'Okay, thanks everyone. I saw most of you got that right, but there was one common mistake: a lot of you forgot that *four* is a multiple of four. Don't forget that the first multiple of any number is the number itself. Let's check you've got that. On your Show-Me Boards, I'd like to see the first five multiples of seven. Keep your boards down this time until I ask everyone to hold them up together.'

Notes

As a rule of thumb, the less students have to write on Show-Me Boards, the easier it is for the teacher to take in information from everyone. With this in mind, if you want students to write an answer that has multiple points, it might be best to get them to write these one at a time, checking boards after each point has been written, rather than have these all crammed onto a board at once.

Multiple-choice questions can minimise how much students have to write. A sea of As, Bs, Cs and Ds should be much more manageable for the teacher to look at than a sea of 10-word sentences.

Show-Me Boards can be a great tool for helping shy students to contribute without necessarily having to speak in front of their peers.

It is a matter of preference as to whether you want students to hold boards up as they are ready or whether you want everyone to wait and hold them up together. Some people argue that if you let students do this as they are ready, some will cheat by looking at other students' boards. That might be true, but staggering boards going up can be useful if the teacher wants to comment on what's written on individual boards or ask students to amend incorrect answers. In any case, over time you should encourage students to see the importance of showing evidence of *their own* understanding, rather than copying a peer's correct (or incorrect) answer.

It can be useful to make a written note of common mistakes you see on boards. These can be built into **Spotlight Assessment Activities**[71] for future lessons.

Sometimes, you might want to 'borrow' a board from a particular student and use this as a specific example from which to make teaching points. For example, you might say to a student, 'Is it okay for me to use this board to make a few teaching points?' Assuming the student agrees, you can talk to the class about what is on the board. For example, you might say, 'Pay particular attention to [this] – that's exactly

---

71 See 'Theme 2: Asking better questions' for further details.

how it should be done' or 'Just watch out for [this] – I saw quite a few of you write that, but it's not quite right.'

If you are worried about students guessing answers, you could get into the habit of asking them to include a 'confidence score' along with their answer. For example, 2 = confident, 1 = I have some doubts and 0 = a guess.

Trusted Technique 3: Chat to a Partner

You ask a question and give students time to talk to a peer about what they are thinking.

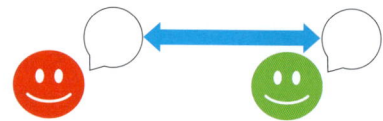

Why use it? (STAR: Spotlight, Thinking, Attention, Responding)

By giving students time to talk, you are also giving them time to think. More than this, you are giving students the opportunity to check their thinking with another student. This can build confidence and increase their willingness to share their answer with the rest of the class. By articulating their thoughts, it can also help them to refine these and uncover the true depth of their understanding.

If you listen in to some of the conversations going on, you can glean formative information about what students know and don't know. You can then respond to this at an appropriate time, such as when you address the class. For example, you might say, 'I heard lots of good discussion there. One thing that I did pick up was that a lot of you were saying [this], but that's not quite right…'

Specific input | Focused reflection | **Deliberate practice**

Suggested steps

1. You ask a question and follow up with a phrase such as:
   - 'Two minutes: chat to a partner.'
   - 'Have a chat about that for 30 seconds.'
2. As students are chatting, you move around the room and listen to some of the conversations, making a mental (or physical) note of any key points.
3. You give a signal for the conversations to stop. For example, you might put up your hand, or you might say, 'Right, everyone stop there, thanks. Full attention back on me.'
4. You address the class and ask selected students to share what they have discussed and/or you summarise key points you heard when listening in.
5. You summarise key takeaway messages so everyone is clear about these.

Example

In a physics lesson...

Teacher 'What do you remember about series and parallel circuits from the past three lessons? Take two minutes and chat to a partner.'

Students chat and the teacher circulates the room, listening to conversations.

Teacher 'Okay, let's stop there. [Waits for silence and full attention.] I heard lots of interesting points being discussed. Could you tell us what you and your partner were discussing, please... Wesley?'

Wesley 'We said that series circuits just have one route, but parallel circuits can have more than one.'

Teacher	'Thanks, Wesley. I actually heard quite a few pairs use the word "route". Gael and Laraine, I think you used a better word. What was it, please, Laraine?'
Laraine	'It was *branches*.'
Teacher	'Right. So, series circuits just have one *branch* but parallel circuits can have more than one. Let's make sure we all use the word "branch" next time.'

Notes

Chat to a Partner can be particularly useful when you are asking an open question that doesn't necessarily have a definitive correct answer. For example, when you want to find out:

- What students already know about something at the start of a lesson or topic.
- What students can remember from a previous lesson.
- What students have understood from a particular section of the current lesson.
- What students' opinions or beliefs are about something.

It is also a useful technique if you want students to think about something that is particularly challenging or complex. Effectively, the technique creates an imaginary safety net for getting things wrong. Students are usually less bothered about getting something wrong in front of the class if they have had a chance to talk to a partner first. Instead of saying, '*I* think…', they can say, '*We* think…'

As well as helping you glean formative information about what students know or don't know, circulating the room during paired discussion should help to keep students on task with what they are discussing. As you circulate the room, it can be useful to have a small notepad to hand so you can jot down key points. With the best will in the world, it can be difficult to remember all of these (even if you think you will).

Trusted Technique 4: Patient Hands

You ask a question and allow hands to go up, but don't choose a student to answer immediately. Instead, you wait and encourage more hands to go up, after which you choose a student with their hand up to answer.

Why use it? (STAR: Spotlight, Thinking, Attention, Responding)

Patient Hands encourages active participation from all students. In other words, it helps push all students to think.

It can stop the most confident students from being the only ones to offer answers. It can also help you gauge how easy or difficult students are finding a question.

Suggested steps

1. You ask a question and wait. Resist any temptation to choose the first (or second or third) student to put their hand up.
2. [Optional.] Give recognition to students who have put their hand up (such as a simile or a nod) but continue to wait. If necessary, encourage more hands to go up by saying things such as 'I'm just going to wait for a few more hands' or 'I can see eight hands up, which is good, but I'd like to see a few more.'

3   Choose a student who has their hand up to answer.

Examples

In a geography lesson...

Teacher   'What is the difference between latitude and longitude? Hands up.'

Two hands go up immediately. You smile at these students but don't choose them to answer. You wait five seconds. More hands go up in this time.

Teacher   'I can see six hands now. Come on, let's have a few more.'

You wait a few seconds longer. More hands go up.

Teacher   [To a student who has their hand up.] 'Carl, you go first.'

Notes

Try to keep a mental note of which students have recently answered questions so you can choose different students to answer in future. If it's always the same students who are chosen, you can frustrate and demotivate others in the class. For example, they can start to think things like 'my teacher only ever asks *them*, so what's the point of me putting up my hand'.

Trusted Technique 5: Cold Call

You ask a question, pause and then name a student to answer, regardless of whether their hand is up or not.

Why use it? (STAR: Spotlight, Thinking, Attention, Responding)

Just because you ask a question, it doesn't mean everyone will think about it. **Cold Call** encourages more students to pay attention and think because *anyone* could be chosen to answer.

It can stop the same students from dominating question/answer exchanges and can help shy and less confident students to participate (so long as you use the technique in a 'warm' way).

Suggested steps

1. You ask a question.
2. You pause.
3. You name a student to answer who may or may not have put up their hand.

Specific input | Focused reflection | **Deliberate practice**

Example

In a maths lesson...

Teacher   'What is nine multiplied by three... [pause] ...Logan?'

Notes

Because students are allowed to put their hands up, this technique is different from 'no hands up' approaches. Allowing students to put their hand up can help you to gauge the difficulty of a question. It can also help create an ethos of enthusiasm and willingness to participate in lessons.[72]

Always try to ask the question, pause, *then* name a student to answer, rather than naming a student *before* asking the question. If you do the latter, you risk other students switching off because they know the question isn't being directed at them.

An extension of this technique is **Chained Cold Call**. With this, multiple students are cold called, one after another. For example, the teacher might say, 'Can you name a prime number between one and 20, please... Jordie?' Jordie says, 'Five,' and then you say, 'Good. Please name another one... Erin.' Erin says, '19,' and you say, 'Good. Let's have another one... Poppy.' This continues for as long as you think there is value.

Cold Call offers a great means for you to control the pace of the lesson.[73] If you want the lesson to have some urgency, you can ask a succession of Cold Call questions, each with just a few seconds' thinking time. If you want to slow things down, you can let students have more thinking time with each question.

---

[72] Taking this to the extreme, some teachers have found a lot of value in asking every student to put their hand up every time a question is asked.

[73] Lemov, D. (2021) *Teach Like a Champion 3.0.*

Contrary to criticisms that are sometimes directed at Cold Call, used correctly (with a warm tone and supportive intentions), the technique is one of the most inclusive questioning strategies available to teachers. Students who are keen to participate but too shy to put up their hand are supported to do so when the teacher 'cold calls' them.

Trusted Technique 6: On the Hook

A student who has recently answered a question is asked another a relatively short time afterwards (as opposed to being 'ticked off as done' and not asked again for an extended period).

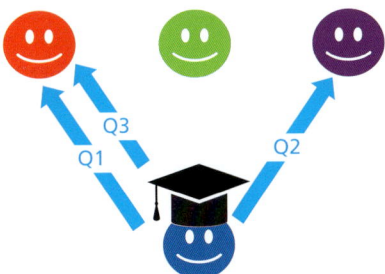

Why use it? (STAR: Spotlight, Thinking, Attention, Responding)

If students believe you are 'working your way around the class', they can switch off once their turn has passed. For example, if there are 30 students in the room, a student who has just been asked a question might believe that the other 29 are going to be asked before they will be again. This technique helps prevent that and holds students' attention.

Specific input | Focused reflection | **Deliberate practice**

Suggested steps

1. You ask a question to student A, which they answer (correctly or incorrectly).
2. You move on to ask at least one other student a question, before coming back to ask student A another question a short time later.

Example

In a science lesson...

Teacher	'Which gas is the most abundant in the Earth's atmosphere... [pause]... Kirsty?'
Kirsty	'Nitrogen.'
Teacher	'Good. Which is the second most abundant gas... Scott?'
Scott	'Oxygen.'
Teacher	'Well done. How much of our atmosphere is made up of oxygen... Laura?'
Laura	'About 20%.'
Teacher	'Good. And what percentage is nitrogen... Kirsty?' [Kirsty is being kept **On the Hook**.]
Kirsty	'Um... I don't know.'
Teacher	[In a warm tone.] 'Did you hear the question?'
Kirsty	'No. Sorry.'
Teacher	[Again, in a warm tone.] 'Okay, well make sure you keep listening. What percentage of the Earth's atmosphere is nitrogen?'
Kirsty	'Just under 80%.'
Teacher	'Well done.'

Notes

Ultimately, we want all students to feel like they are *always* **On the Hook**. In other words, we want them to understand that anyone could be asked a question *at any time*, so it is important that everyone keeps paying attention.

To use the technique effectively, you usually need to make a mental note about who is answering questions. If you find this difficult, make a physical note. For example, you could write things on your class seating plan.

As with almost all aspects of teaching, use of a 'warm tone' is important with this technique. The reaction you get to the question 'Were you paying attention?' will be very different depending on the tone you use. A degree of warmth will likely lead to a cooperative response. A tone of frustration or annoyance will often lead to students becoming huffy, petulant and uncooperative.

The wording you choose is also important. For example, compare the following two phrases and ask yourself which is likely to come across as warmer:

- 'Pay attention, Holly.'
- 'It's important you keep paying attention, Holly.'

Trusted Technique 7: Choral Response

You ask a question that all students are expected to answer verbally at the same time.

Why use it? (STAR: Spotlight, Thinking, Attention, Responding)

This technique gets all students to participate actively (i.e. to think) and addresses the issue of some students choosing to be passive in their learning. In doing so, it helps hold attention.

Suggested steps

1. You ask a question and follow this up with a phrase such as:
   - 'Everyone, together.'
   - 'Choral response.' (You have taught them what this means.)
   - 'On three, everyone.'

   Alternatively, you introduce the question by saying something like 'This is a choral response question.'
2. As students answer you scan the room, checking for 100% participation.
3. If you see any students who aren't participating, you draw attention to this, saying something like:
   - 'A few of us didn't participate with that one. Let's go again.'
   - 'I need to see *everyone* participating – that's really important. Let's have another go.'

Specific input | Focused reflection | **Deliberate practice**

Students then have another go.

4 If you hear any incorrect answers, you draw attention to these, making the correct answer clear to everyone.
5 You ask the question again, making it clear you are looking for everyone to get the answer correct this time.

Example

In an English language lesson with the words 'noun', 'verb' and 'adjective' written on the board as the three options for students to choose from...

Teacher   'In the sentence "Greg suddenly hit the ball", which word is the verb? *Everyone*, together.'

The teacher listens and scans the room as 25 students answer in unison. They note that two students don't answer and that there were at least four incorrect answers.

Teacher   'That wasn't bad, but I heard a few incorrect answers, and I saw two of you who didn't say anything. The correct answer is "hit" because this tells us what Greg was *doing*. Remember: verbs are *doing* words. Let's try another example together. I'll be looking for 100% participation this time.'

Notes

Used well, **Choral Response** can help to bring about 'three Es' of great teaching: engagement, energy and enthusiasm. As well as encouraging all students to participate actively, the technique helps ensure all students experience success and feel they are a part of a shared learning community, with everyone's learning being important and moving forward together.

Specific input | Focused reflection | **Deliberate practice**

If you are drawing attention to participation levels that are below 100%, as far as possible, try to avoid singling out particular students who aren't participating. For example, don't say: 'I saw everyone participating except Jamie.' That's not going to make Jamie feel good. Instead, try to use generic phrases, such as 'Let's have another go with everyone participating this time.' If you need to, you can have a quiet word with Jamie later.

Power up your questioning

Theme 4: Responding better to students' answers
*– so you can explore their thinking
and push learning forward*

Overview

Common Pitfalls	Power-Up Prompts	Trusted Techniques
1. Not considering students' likely incorrect answers to preplanned questions. 2. Accepting or correcting answers without exploring the understanding beneath them. 3. Accepting incorrect or partially incorrect answers as correct. 4. Allowing students to opt out.	Through careful listening, teaching engages with students' answers, including the specific detail of these. Students who can't answer questions are supported and challenged to learn what they need to answer these in future. ■ To what extent is this typically true? ■ What do you currently do to ensure this? ■ What could you do to make this *even better*?	Drill Down Stick with You Homing In Push for Perfect Coax It Out Return Visit Phone a Friend Go Again Instruct Memorisation

Common Pitfall 1: Not considering students' likely incorrect answers to preplanned questions

Just as important as planning key targeted questions in advance of lessons (as discussed in Theme 2) is considering the *most likely answers* students will give to these during a lesson. In particular, it is important to consider the *incorrect* answers students might (and probably will) give, based on our knowledge of common mistakes they tend to make and common misconceptions they have. The more prepared we are for mistakes and misconceptions, the more likely we are to spot and respond well to these as they arise.

For example, you might plan to ask students to draw a diagram showing how particles are arranged in solids, liquids and gases. A correct student response would look like this (which is obviously important for you to be aware of):

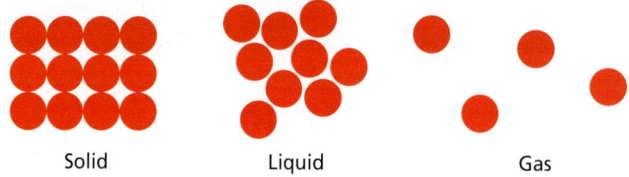

Solid   Liquid   Gas

An incorrect student response would look like this:

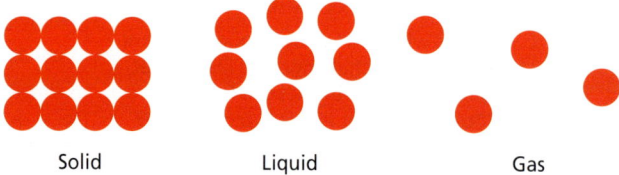

Solid   Liquid   Gas

A common mistake that students make is show spaces that are too large between particles in a liquid. If you have considered this in advance of the lesson, you are more likely to be looking out for it during the activity. Accordingly, this mistake is less likely to go unnoticed and uncorrected during the lesson.

Become a lighthouse

Effectively, you act as a lighthouse, constantly scanning the classroom on the lookout for mistakes, so that important teaching points can be made from them.[74] We don't want students' learning to crash on the rocks.

> **Pitfall Avoidance Principle**
>
> As part of lesson planning, consider the mistakes and misconceptions that are likely to accompany preplanned questions, including *how you intend to respond to these*.

---

74 Doug Lemov discusses this as 'Plan for Error'.

Lure them out

If teachers get into the habit of making notes (mental or physical) about common mistakes students make with questions, they can build these into future **Spotlight Assessment Activities**, explanations or modelling. By doing so, misconceptions that might have otherwise slipped by unchecked can be highlighted and addressed with all students.

For example, you might know that a common misconception students have in science is that liquids need to boil to evaporate. Rather than leave it to chance as to whether this is highlighted and discussed in a lesson, it would be better to ask a question specifically designed to draw attention to this misconception, such as a Concept Cartoon:

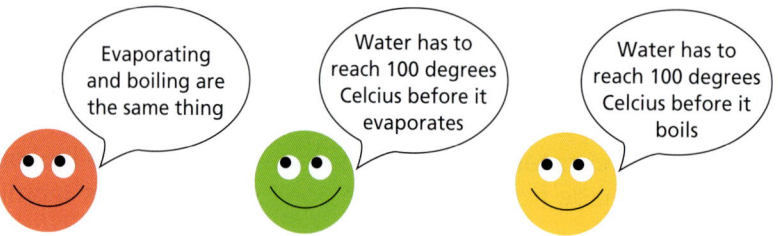

Pitfall Avoidance Principle

Preplan questions that deliberately target common mistakes and misconceptions.

Common Pitfall 2: Accepting or correcting answers without exploring the understanding beneath them

The answers students give to our questions should be thought of as icebergs: what sits beneath answers is as important – if not more important – than the answers themselves. We discussed this in Theme 2 in relation to surface knowledge and deeper understanding:

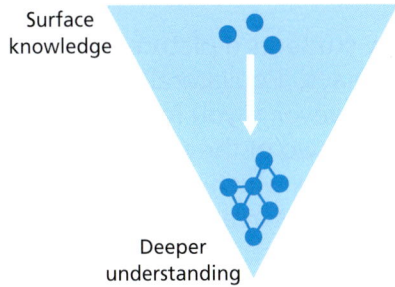

With this in mind, an important part of a teacher's job is to ensure sufficient time is spent exploring the deeper understanding that sits below surface knowledge using techniques such as **Drill Down** and **Stick with You**. Let's explore this.

Correct answers, by accident

Sometimes, students answer questions correctly but by accident – they either guess or they give a correct answer based on a misconception.

For example, imagine you ask, 'What is the capital of Canada?' and a student answers, 'Ottawa' (which is correct). The temptation might be to say, 'Good, that's right,' and move on. However, doing so would miss

Specific input | Focused reflection | Deliberate practice

a valuable opportunity to explore *what sits beneath* their answer. If you followed up by asking 'How sure are you?' and the student says 'Very sure' or 'I'm certain', this is valuable formative information to have uncovered because it suggests they haven't guessed. If they say 'Not very sure – it was a guess', this is equally valuable. Alternatively, you might follow up by saying, 'A lot of people think the answer is Montreal or Quebec. Is there anything you do to help you remember the answer is Ottawa?' The student might say, 'No, I just remember' or they might say, 'Yes, I remember that the last letter is the same as the last letter of "Canada", and that helps me.' Either way, again, both responses would be valuable to know. Students' strategies to remember things should be useful for other students to know too.

As a second example, imagine you show students a picture of a triangle with three equal sides and ask, 'What type of triangle is this?' A student says, 'Equilateral' (which is correct), and the temptation might be for you to say 'Good' and move on. However, if you follow this question up by asking 'Why do you think that?' and the student says, 'Because two of the sides are the same length,' you know that they have got the right answer *but for the wrong reason*, which needs to be addressed. If we don't make time to 'weed out' and address misconceptions like this in a robust way, they will almost certainly lead to future problems.

Exploring incorrect answers

The previous examples related to correct answers that students give, but getting beneath the surface of *incorrect* answers can be even more important. Counterintuitively, teachers should be just as excited about getting incorrect answers as correct ones, due to the formative opportunities these create in teaching. Rather than getting frustrated by incorrect answers, our mindset should be: 'Great! This is a golden opportunity for me to drill down and find out what's sitting beneath.'[75]

---

75 Though it should be appreciated that this is sometimes easier said than done.

For example, imagine a student said that they thought Quebec is the capital of Canada (which is wrong). If you replied, 'No, it's actually Ottawa,' and moved on, you have corrected the surface knowledge but not in a way that really addresses it. You have pulled out the top of the weed but left the roots in place. As a result, if asked this question again in future (perhaps a month later), there is every chance the student will again say 'Quebec', because they have forgotten your correction and reverted to what they originally thought. Effectively, the weed has regrown.

Had you spent a little time helping the student devise a memory aid to remember the correct answer (such as the one about the letter 'a' at the end of both the capital city and the country), you would have helped them develop new knowledge connections, making it more likely that the correct answer would be remembered. **Addressing mistakes in an effective way often requires more than the teacher simply telling students the correct answer.**

As a second example, imagine you ask, 'Is calcium a metal or a non-metal?' and a student answers, 'A non-metal' (which is a common mistake). You could say, 'No, it's a metal,' but as we have just discussed, this wouldn't be great teaching because there is a good chance the student will answer 'non-metal' again in the future. However, if you follow up by saying, 'Why do you think that?', you create the opportunity to address deeper understanding. Perhaps the student says, 'Because I know there is calcium in milk and teeth, and these aren't metal.' This exposes an important misconception that needs to be addressed. If this student has it, there's a good chance others will as well. However, if you hadn't taken a few more seconds to dig a little deeper, you would never know that. Now, having found out *why* the student thought this, you can address the underlying issue (which, in this example, might involve you showing students a photo of calcium, so they can see it is a metal, or explaining that it is actually compounds of calcium – rather than the element itself – that are present in milk and teeth).

Correcting answers in a superficial way

Sometimes when students give an incorrect answer to questions that involve a binary choice – such as true or false or 'Is calcium a metal or a non-metal?' – teachers can fall into the trap of correcting these superficially, saying something like 'No, it's the other one' or 'Try again…'. Students then pick the alternative answer, which is correct, and the teacher moves on, happy with this.

However, just because a teacher gets a correct answer in the end, **it doesn't mean students have learned anything**. Handing students correct answers on a plate doesn't tend to do their learning any favours. By removing the requirement for them to think, we have taken away the very experience that is most likely to help them learn.

It's fine to tell students that an answer is wrong, but we also need to push and support them to think about *why* this is, and *how to remember* the correct answer. We mustn't remove the healthy cognitive struggle that is usually so important for learning.

Pitfall Avoidance Principle

Make explorative follow-up questions the norm, asking these more often than not.

❌ Question → Correct answer → Accept and move on

❌ Question → Incorrect answer → Teacher corrects with no explanation

✅ Question → Correct answer → **At least one explorative follow-up question** → Move on

✅ Question → Incorrect answer → **At least one explorative follow-up question** → Explain correct answer

---

Specific input | Focused reflection | Deliberate practice

Common Pitfall 3: Accepting incorrect or partially incorrect answers as correct

As teachers, naturally, we want our students to be successful. When we ask them questions, we hope they will answer correctly, in part because we know this will make them feel good. However, as we have just discussed, we also know it is **just as important for students to sometimes get things wrong**. If students are getting every question we ask correct, we probably aren't creating the desirable difficulties we need to be.

Accepting this, the trap teachers need to avoid is letting our desire for students to be successful trump the need to make them aware when they aren't. If a student gives an incorrect or partially incorrect answer to a question, we need to make this clear to them, for example, by **Homing In**. If we don't, all we ultimately do is damage their learning.

For example, imagine a teacher asks students to 'Empty Your Brain on climate change'. They give everyone four minutes to write everything they know about this topic before asking for responses to be shared with the class. One student volunteers the answer 'It's to do with carbon dioxide and the ozone layer'. 'Great!' says the teacher. 'Who would like to go next?'

The student was right to suggest that climate change has something to do with carbon dioxide, but incorrect to say it is to do with the ozone layer. However, the teacher did not highlight or address this. As a result, this student – and potentially others who heard their answer or also thought this – has been left with an uncorrected misconception.

Why do teachers accept incorrect and partially correct answers?

Beyond our desire for students to be successful, there are three further reasons why teachers can sometimes ignore incorrect or partially correct answers to questions. These are because:

Specific input | Focused reflection | Deliberate practice

1. They don't think there is enough time to explore and address what a student has said, so they move on regardless, hoping it won't be too much of an issue in future (but it probably will).
2. They think the concepts that underpin the correct answer are too complex for students to understand, or that there is too big a gap from their existing knowledge, so they avoid the issue (only for it to come back to bite them further down the line).
3. They haven't listened carefully enough to the *precise detail* of what a student has said, so they miss the fact that something was wrong.

None of these reasons are good enough for us to excuse. It is an essential part of our job to make it clear to students when they are wrong. Because we *know* that many students are going to get many of our questions wrong, we need to plan lesson time accordingly. Being honest, we are doing them a disservice if we don't. We also need to make sure that we listen carefully to what students are telling us in their answers. Answers that are 'along the right lines' or 'getting close' are rarely good enough to accept without doing something about. We need to **Push for Perfect**.

Pitfall Avoidance Principle

Be on the lookout for mistakes in students' answers, no matter how small. When you spot these, draw students' attention to them and help students understand why they are wrong.

 Question → Incorrect or partially correct answer → Ignore or gloss over and move on

 Question → Incorrect or partially correct answer → **Make mistakes clear, including why**

Common Pitfall 4: Allowing students to opt out

Given the chance, students will often take advantage of any opportunity you give them not to think or not to share an answer to a question in front of their peers. In other words, they look for opportunities to opt out of the teaching and learning process.[76]

The reasons they opt out of thinking include 1) thinking is hard work,[77] and 2) there are often more interesting things to think about.[78] The reasons they opt out of sharing answers in front of peers include 1) they don't want to get an answer wrong, and 2) because it's not 'cool' to do that. The easy and most attractive option for students can often be to say 'I don't know' when asked a question, even if they do know or could remember, given a bit of a push. How should a teacher react to this?

What should I do if a student says 'I don't know'?

If a student says 'I don't know', the easiest thing can be to say 'Okay' and answer the question ourselves or ask another student to answer. However, doing so gives the student who said 'I don't know' a **thinking get-out** (as discussed in Theme 3) and will do little to help their learning.

The best thing you could do to help the student's learning would be to push and support them to arrive at a correct answer. Trusted Techniques that can help include **Coax It Out**, **Return Visit**, **Phone a Friend**, **Go Again** and **Instruct Memorisation**. A common thread that runs through each of these techniques is that if a student says they don't know (or they get an answer wrong), that is usually fine, so long as they *do know* the next time the question is asked. They aren't allowed to opt out of learning.

---

76 Lemov, D. (2021) *Teach Like a Champion 3.0.*
77 Willingham, D.T. (2009) *Why Don't Students Like School?*
78 Such as TV, music, sport, friends…

> **Pitfall Avoidance Principle**
>
> If a student says 'I don't know' or gets an answer wrong, either:
> - Stick with them to try to tease out the correct answer, or
> - Go back to them once they have had the opportunity to hear the correct answer to make sure they know it now.
>
> ❌ Question → 'I don't know' → Student told correct answer → Lesson moves on
>
> ✅ Question → 'I don't know' → **Student pushed and supported to answer, which they give**
>
> ✅ Question → 'I don't know' → Student told correct answer → Lesson moves on → **Student asked again a short time later**

Be careful not to make 'I don't know' the norm

All of this said, we should be cautious when it comes to accepting 'I don't know' responses. There is a fine line between making this acceptable *periodically* (when students genuinely don't know) and making this acceptable *regularly* (with students just taking the easier option not to bother trying).

For example, if a teacher keeps saying 'It's okay to say you don't know', they shouldn't be surprised when they see a set of **Show-Me Boards** that look like this:[79]

---

79 IDK stands for 'I don't know'.

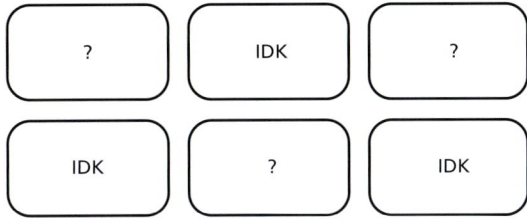

As we have said, there is a fine line to tread, but we mustn't allow thinking get-outs to sabotage learning.

Power-Up Prompts

Through careful listening, teaching engages with students' answers, including the specific detail of these.

Students who can't answer questions are supported and challenged to learn what they need to answer these in future.

1. To what extent is this typically true?
2. What do you currently do to ensure this?
3. What could you do to make this *even better*?

Deeper-Thinking Questions

Reflection/coaching questions for *before* a lesson:

1. What steps do you plan to take in this lesson to ensure you are listening carefully to students' answers?
2. Are there particular Trusted Techniques you will be focusing on?

Specific input | **Focused reflection** | Deliberate practice

3. If so, what specific aspects of these techniques will you consciously be trying to do well?
4. What do you plan to do in this lesson if you discover a student can't answer a question correctly?
5. What do you plan to do in this lesson if you find multiple students can't answer a question correctly?

Reflection/coaching questions for *after* a lesson:
1. To what extent do you feel you listened carefully to students' answers?
2. To what extent do you feel you responded well to students' answers?
3. Can you give a specific example of a student's answer you think you responded well to, including why you think that?
4. Were there particular Trusted Techniques you were using to help with this?
5. How successful do you think these were?
6. Is there anything you think you could have done to make these more successful?
7. Are there any other techniques you could use to make this even better?
8. How well do you think you responded when you found out students couldn't answer a question correctly?
9. Do you think you did enough to check that students who couldn't answer a question first time round learned what they needed to answer it correctly the next time?
10. Are there any other techniques you could use to make this even better?

Trusted Technique 1: Drill Down

A student's (correct or incorrect) answer to a question is followed-up with at least one open question to explore their thinking. For example:

- 'Why do you think that?'
- 'Could you say a little more about that?'
- 'What makes you so sure of that?'
- 'Okay, so you're saying [this], but would it be okay to say [this]?'
- 'What do you do to help remember that?'

Why use it? (STAR: Spotlight, Thinking, Attention, Responding)

Follow-up questions encourage students to think harder about particular things. This helps establish knowledge connections and strengthen memory. They can also help you to find out if a student has arrived at a correct answer via a misconception or guess. It is equally important for you to find out the reasons students have answered incorrectly.

Suggested steps

1 You ask a student a question, which they answer (correctly or incorrectly).
2 You ask *at least one* open question to explore their thinking further.

Example

In a modern studies lesson...

Teacher 'As part of our discussion about democracy, we have been talking about press freedom. What do we mean by a "free press"... [pause]... Melissa?'

Melissa 'It means newspapers can say what they want about things.'

Teacher 'Just newspapers?'

Melissa 'No, it means things like TV as well.'

Teacher 'Okay, good. So can you tell us a bit more about that, please?'

Melissa 'Well, I know that the government isn't allowed to tell the press what they're allowed to say or not.'

Teacher 'That's right. And do you think that's a good or a bad thing?'

Melissa 'A good thing.'

Teacher 'Why?'

The exchange continues with a few further follow-up questions before a different student is asked a question.

Notes

Asking questions that involve **comparisons** can offer a useful means to **Drill Down** into students' understanding. For example:

- Why is seven a prime number but eight isn't?
- Why is a spider an invertebrate but a camel isn't?

Specific input | Focused reflection | **Deliberate practice**

To maximise the learning experience for everyone, it is important to have established a classroom culture in which every student listens carefully to everyone else. You don't want other students switching off during your drilling down exchange. To ensure everyone is listening, you might also use the **Bounce** technique (see Theme 5) as you are drilling. For example, you might say, 'And do you agree with what Melissa has just said… Emma?'

Trusted Technique 2: Stick with You

A student's (correct or incorrect) answer to a question is followed-up with at least one closed question designed to find out more about the specific things they know or understand.

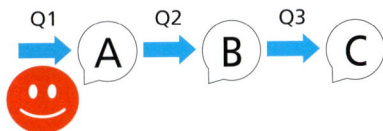

Why use it? (STAR: Spotlight, Thinking, Attention, Responding)

This technique is useful for helping students to think harder about particular content, developing knowledge connections and strengthening memory. It helps the teacher to glean more formative information about a student's learning than a single question would have.

Suggested steps

1 You ask a student a question, which they answer correctly.
2 You ask then ask *at least one* further closed question, designed to explore what they know and understand in *a specific way*.

Example

In a biology lesson...

Teacher 'Can you remind us what the reactants and products in photosynthesis are please... Neil?'

Neil 'Carbon dioxide and water are the reactants; oxygen and sugar are the products.'

Teacher 'Good. And sticking with you, could you tell us what else needs to be present for photosynthesis to happen, please?'

Neil 'Sunlight.'

Teacher 'Good. And what chemical do plants have that helps them trap sunlight?'

Neil 'Chlorophyll.'

Teacher 'Perfect. Well done.'

Notes

Stick with You is subtly different to **Drill Down**. Stick with You uses closed questions to get students to say more about what they know and understand; Drill Down uses open questions to explore the reasons why a student has given a particular answer.

Trusted Technique 3: Homing In

A student gives a partially correct or close-to-correct answer to a question and the teacher supports them to make it correct.

Specific input | Focused reflection | **Deliberate practice**

Why use it? (STAR: Spotlight, Thinking, Attention, Responding)

Drawing attention to particular mistakes should make it less likely that these occur in future. Students often know and understand more than their initial answers suggest. **Homing In** gives them the chance to 'redraft' and improve their answers.

Students coming up with their own improvements should be more beneficial to their learning than the teacher doing this for them. The technique requires the student to do the cognitive work, meaning their learning is more *active*.

Suggested steps

1. You ask a question and a student gives a partially correct answer or an incorrect one that is close.
2. You say something to indicate that the answer isn't perfectly correct. For example, you might say, 'Nearly, but there was one word in that answer that wasn't quite right. Can you think what it was?'
3. You give the student the opportunity to improve their answer.
4. If the answer is now correct, you recognise this. If not, you give the student one more chance to improve it or you ask another student to do the same.
5. Once a correct answer is given, you make the specifics of this clear.

Example

In a maths lesson, the following expression is presented to students:

$a \times a = 2a$

Teacher   'Is this true or false? On Show-Me Boards please, everyone.'

Everyone writes an answer, some of which say 'T' and some say 'F'.

Specific input | Focused reflection | **Deliberate practice**

Teacher	'Jamie, you've said false. Can you tell us why you think that, please?'
Jamie	'Because it should be "a" times "a" equals "a" with a subscripted two.'
Teacher	'Nearly. Are you sure you mean subscripted?'
Jamie	'No, sorry. I mean superscripted.'
Teacher	'That's better. Superscripted means the number appears in the top-right, which is correct.'

Notes

This technique relies on the teacher listening carefully to what students say. It also requires the teacher to resist any temptation to gloss over mistakes, however small these might be.

Trusted Technique 4: Push for Perfect

A student gives an answer that is good and, arguably, acceptable, but the teacher pushes them to arrive at an even better one.

Why use it? (STAR: Spotlight, Thinking, Attention, Responding)

Students will only tend to jump as high as we set the bar. The higher our expectations, the more likely students will give great answers to questions.

A student's first answer to a question can often be thought of as an initial draft. Students will often be appreciative of the opportunity to refine and improve their answers. They just need to be given the chance.

Students coming up with their own improvements should be more beneficial to their learning than the teacher doing this for them. The technique requires the student to do the cognitive work, meaning their learning is more *active*.

Suggested steps

1. You ask a question and a student gives an answer that is good, but could be *even better*.
2. You say something to indicate that.
3. You give the student the opportunity to improve their answer.
4. If there is improvement, you recognise this. If not, you give the student one more chance to improve it or you ask another student to do the same.
5. Once you reach the 'perfect' answer, you make the specific aspects of this clear.

Example

In a science lesson...

Teacher 'What is the role of the stomach in digestion... Molly?'

Molly 'It has acid and other chemicals in it, which help breakdown food.' [This is correct, but there could be more detail.]

Teacher 'That's pretty good, but I think you could improve the answer a little. What is *the name* of the acid?'

Specific input | Focused reflection | **Deliberate practice**

Molly	'Hydrochloric.'
Teacher	'Good. And now let's improve "chemicals", because I think you can do better than that.'
Molly	'I'm not sure.'
Teacher	'It begins with an E.'
Molly	'I'm not sure.'
Teacher	'Okay. Someone else. Let's see some hands.'

There is thinking time. Hands go up.

Teacher	'Justin, what do you think?'
Justin	'It's enzymes that are in the stomach.'
Teacher	'Well done. Right, everyone, on a Show-Me Board, I'd like you to write me the *perfect answer* to the question "What is the role of the stomach in digestion?" Go!'

The teacher scans the room to read what students have written on boards.

Teacher	'Okay, thanks. The two key things I'm looking to be mentioned are hydrochloric acid and enzymes. I can see that almost everyone wrote those. Next time, remember to include both.'

Notes

Push for Perfect is essentially a variation of **Homing In**. However, whereas that technique is about partially correct and almost correct answers, this one is about answers that are correct but could be *even better*.

Specific input | Focused reflection | **Deliberate practice**

At the end of a lengthy exchange such as that given in the example, it is important that something is done to pull together the key points in a summary. Otherwise, we risk students being left confused or unclear about what these are.

Trusted Technique 5: Coax It Out

A student gets an answer wrong or says they don't know, so the teacher rewords the question, breaks it down into a series of sub-questions or uses hints or cues to try to tease out the correct answer (rather than tell the student what this is or ask another student to answer).

Why use it? (STAR: Spotlight, Thinking, Attention, Responding)

Often, the learning is in the struggle. That's why we talk about 'desirable difficulties' as being so important. By telling a student the correct answer or by getting another student to do the same, we create a 'thinking get-out' for the student who couldn't answer. It should be better for the students' learning to support them to arrive at a good answer themselves. **Coax It Out** can bridge the gap between struggle and success.

Suggested steps

1   You ask a question and a student says 'I don't know' or gets the answer wrong.

2 You do one of three things:
  i Reframe i.e. word the question in a different way.
  ii Break the question down into a series of sub-questions, designed to lead the student to the correct answer to the original question.
  iii Offer one or more hints or cues (for example: 'It starts with the letter M' or 'It rhymes with "well"').
3 If the student still can't answer the question, you should move on to ask another student. As you do this, you could say something like, 'I can see you've tried hard, but you're still stuck – that's okay. Let's see who else can help and I'll come back to you.'
4 A short time after a correct answer has been given, you ask the student who couldn't answer again to make sure they can now.

Example

In a maths lesson, with the following rectangle drawn on the board...

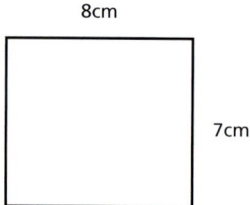

Teacher   'What is the area of the rectangle... Elsie?'
Elsie   'I don't know.'
Teacher   'Okay. Well, is there anything you do know about calculating the area of a rectangle?'

Elsie	'No.'
Teacher	'Okay. Well, if I told you it has something to do with either adding or multiplying numbers, would that help?'
Elsie	'Um… do you multiply the sides together?'
Teacher	'You don't think that you *add them*?'
Elsie	'No, I think that would give you the perimeter.'
Teacher	'Well done. So, keep going. What happens if you multiply the sides together?'
Elsie	'You get 54.'
Teacher	'Try again.'
Elsie	'You get 56.'
Teacher	'Perfect. And what would the units be?'
Elsie	'Centimetres.'
Teacher	'Try again.'

There is a pause for five seconds.

Elsie	'Centimetres squared.'
Teacher	'Spot on. Well done. So please tell us the correct answer.'
Elsie	'56 centimetres squared.'

Notes

When using this technique, be mindful of using a supportive and encouraging tone of voice. There is more than one way to say 'try again' and not all of them come across as kind (which is, of course, how we should be trying to come across).

Trusted Technique 6: Return Visit

A student gets an answer wrong or says they don't know, so the teacher asks someone else, who answers correctly. A short time later, the teacher goes back to the student who didn't know to ask them the same question (or one that is very similar).

Why use it? (STAR: Spotlight, Thinking, Attention, Responding)

It is okay for students not to know the answer to a question, so long as they *do know* the next time the question is asked. **Return Visit** helps ensure that they do.

Suggested steps

1. You ask a question and a student says 'I don't know' or gets the answer wrong.
2. [Optional.] You push a little, saying something like 'It's got something to do with...' or 'Think back to what we were talking about yesterday', but the student still doesn't know.
3. You ask another student who answers correctly.

Specific input | Focused reflection | **Deliberate practice**

4   You go back to the student who couldn't answer, either immediately or a short time later, and ask them the same question or one that is very similar.

5   If the student now answers correctly, you move on. If not, you give the student another chance to hear the correct answer, then repeat step 4.

Example

In a science lesson…

Teacher 'Remind us what the three essential elements found in fertilisers are, please… Fraser.'

Fraser 'I don't know.'

Teacher 'Okay. Well, one of them begins with N and the other two begin with P.'

Fraser 'I don't know.'

Teacher 'Okay. Robbie, do you know?'

Robbie 'Nitrogen, potassium and phosphorus.'

Teacher 'Well done. Okay, so it's important that everyone knows this because it's knowledge we'll keep referring back to in this topic. Just remind us what the three elements are, please, Fraser.'

Fraser 'Um… Nitrogen… Potassium… and, um… I don't know.'

Teacher 'Well nitrogen and potassium *are* right. But you need to know all three and Robbie *did just tell us those*. What was the other one, please… Nathan?'

Nathan 'Phosphorus.'

Teacher 'That's right: phosphorus. Nitrogen, potassium and phosphorus are the three essential elements that we find in all fertilisers. I'm going to check everyone knows that using Show-Me Boards later in the lesson.'

Notes

Obviously, we aren't trying to embarrass or humiliate any student with this technique. We're simply trying to help students learn the things they need to. If we didn't care about their learning, we wouldn't ask them again. But of course we *do* care, and that's why it's so important to make the **Return Visit**.

Whether you choose to tell students you will be coming back to them is a matter of professional judgement. If you've created a culture in which students know you are likely to do that, you shouldn't need to tell them – they should be ready for it.

In the example, the teacher only left a few seconds before returning. However, it is sometimes better to leave it a bit longer to avoid a parrot-fashion response. If we do leave more time, it's important that we remember to go back to the student again. Making a written note to do that can be helpful (so long as you remember to look back at the note!).

Another way to avoid parrot-fashion responses is to ask the student a slightly different question on our return. For example, if you ask a student to give an example of a metaphor and they say 'I don't know', you could go to a different student and get a correct answer, and then go back to the original student and ask for a different example.

Return Visit can be powerful when used alongside **Show-Me Boards**. For example, imagine a class have been asked to write a possible pH number for an alkali on Show-Me Boards. Some examples of what the teacher sees are as follows:[80]

---

80 What the teacher would be hoping to see are numbers above 7 but less than 15.

Specific input | Focused reflection | **Deliberate practice**

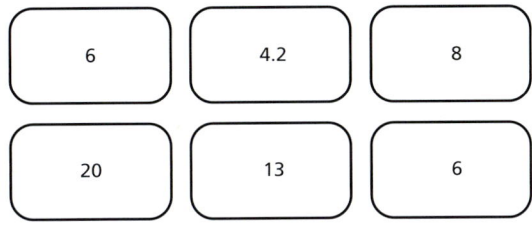

Seeing that some of the class have got this wrong, the teacher does something to address this. For example, they might ask a student who got the answer correct to explain why they chose the answer they did, or they might give feedback themselves, making clear which answers are correct and incorrect. However, *they wouldn't leave it at that*. Rather, at some point soon after, they would ask students the same or a very similar question, because they want to see evidence that all students can now answer this question correctly. For example, they might ask students to write a possible pH number for an alkali on Show-Me Boards again, but everyone has to write a different number to the one they did last time (including students who had previously answered the question correctly).

Trusted Technique 7: Phone a Friend

A student gets an answer wrong or says they don't know, so the teacher allows them to choose another student to answer. A short time later, the teacher goes back to the student who didn't know to check they do now.

Specific input | Focused reflection | **Deliberate practice**

Why use it? (STAR: Spotlight, Thinking, Attention, Responding)

Phone a Friend keeps the requirement to answer questions correctly *with students*. This helps ensure there is a 'desirable difficulty' and reinforces the teacher's expectations that students listen to each other's answers, so that learning is collaborative.

Suggested steps

1. You ask a question and a student says 'I don't know' or gets the answer wrong.
2. [Optional.] You push a little, saying something like 'It's got something to do with…' or 'Think back to what we were talking about yesterday', but the student still doesn't know.
3. You say, 'Would you like to phone a friend?'
4. The student nominates another student to answer.
5. If this student answers correctly, you move on. If not, another friend can be nominated.
6. A short time after a correct answer has been given, you go back to the student who didn't know and ask them the same question or one that is similar.

Example

In a maths lesson…

Teacher	'What is −4 × 3… Max?'
Max	'I don't know.'
Teacher	'Are you sure? I remember you answering a question like this in our last lesson.'
Max	'Sorry, I'm not sure.'

Specific input | Focused reflection | **Deliberate practice**

Teacher	'Okay. Well, phone a friend.'
Max	'I'll phone Erin.'
Teacher	'Okay, Erin. Can you help?'
Erin	'Yes. It's −12.'
Teacher	'Thanks, Erin. Can you explain how you arrived at that answer, please?'

Erin explains her thinking.

Teacher	'That's very good. Right, Max, back to you. I'm going to ask you a very similar question and, based on what Erin has just explained, I'm hoping you'll be able to answer it. What is −2 × 4? I'd like everyone to take a minute to work that out, but Max, I'm going to come to you first.'

Notes

As shown in the example, the technique can get the whole class to think, even if only a few students are chosen to answer.

Don't let the same student (or group of students) always get chosen as the 'friend'. If you need to, intervene and insist that someone else is chosen.

Trusted Technique 8: Go Again

The teacher discovers that a significant number of students can't answer a question that they are expected to be able to answer. The teacher explains what the answer should be and then asks the same question, or one that is similar, a short time later. The expectation is that everyone will now get this correct. (If they don't, the teacher uses the technique **Instruct Memorisation**.)

Why use it? (STAR: Spotlight, Thinking, Attention, Responding)

Not being able to answer a question is okay, so long as students can answer correctly the next time it is asked. This technique makes this expectation clear and encourages students to take ownership of their learning.

Suggested steps

1 You ask a question that *multiple students* are required to answer, but none of them can.
2 You let students know what the correct answer should be (and why).
3 You then ask the same question, or one that is very similar, involving the same students.
4 If multiple students still can't answer it, you do further reteaching. If the class is split in terms of who can answer correctly and who can't, you let students know what the correct answer should be (and why), and then ask another similar question.
5 You repeat step 4 until *at least 80%* of the class can answer correctly, making a note of who can't so you can do individual or small-group reteaching with them at a later point in the lesson.

Specific input | Focused reflection | **Deliberate practice**

Example

In an English language lesson...

Teacher 'On your show-me boards, write a short sentence that includes an adjective, and underline the adjective. You have one minute and then I'll ask everyone to hold their boards up at the same time.'

The teacher waits as students write answers. After 60 seconds, they ask everyone to hold up their boards. Out of a class of 25 students, only four have answered correctly.

Teacher 'Okay, I can see that most of you struggled with that. Julie, Jason, Claire and Phillipa – well done. You all did this well. Phillipa, could you remind the class what an adjective is, please?'

Phillipa 'It's a word that tells us more about a noun.'

Teacher 'Thank you. Everyone, let's look at what Phillipa has written on her board.'

The teacher holds up the board for everyone to see, which looks as follows:

> The flower is <u>beautiful</u>.

Specific input | Focused reflection | **Deliberate practice**

Teacher	'Phillipa has written "The flower is beautiful" and has underlined the word beautiful. "Beautiful" is telling us more about the noun in the sentence. What is the noun, please… Suzanne?'
Suzanne	'Flower.'
Teacher	'That's right. So, the adjective – *beautiful* – is telling us more about the noun – *flower*. I would like everyone to rub out what they just wrote on their boards and give me a new example of a short sentence with an adjective, underlining the adjective.

The class does this, and the teacher sees 18 correct answers.

Teacher	'That's much better, I can see almost all of you have got that right this time. However, there are still a few of you who haven't. Christine, I want you to talk us through your answer and then everyone is going to have another go.'

Christine does this and the teacher makes further teaching points. Everyone has another go and 23 out of 25 students get the answer correct.

Teacher	'Very well done everyone. That's a big improvement. There were just a couple of you who are still struggling. That's fine. I'm going to come and work with you both later in the lesson.'

Notes

As we will discuss in more detail in Theme 6, the 80% Success Rule can be useful to guide your decisions about when to move on.

When you are asking the class to **Go Again**, the worry can often be that you are wasting the time of the students who have already proven they can answer a question. However, that's not usually true, especially when they are generating different examples. Usually, there is real benefit to students going again because it results in *overlearning*.[81] Essentially, the memory being created becomes *even stronger* than it would otherwise have been, meaning it is even less likely to be forgotten in the future. Beyond this, students usually get a lot of satisfaction out of getting things right. Giving them multiple opportunities to do this isn't usually something they will complain about, so long as they feel their learning is developing as the lesson goes on.

Trusted Technique 9: Instruct Memorisation

The teacher discovers that a significant number of students can't answer a question that they are expected to be able to answer. The teacher tells students that they need to learn the correct answer within a set period (for example, by the next lesson) and that they will be asked the question again. The teacher asks the question again at a future point.

---

81   Rosenshine, B. (2012) 'Principles of instruction.'

Specific input | Focused reflection | **Deliberate practice**

Why use it? (STAR: Spotlight, Thinking, Attention, Responding)

Not being able to answer a question is okay, so long as students can answer it the next time it is asked. This technique makes this expectation clear and encourages students to take ownership of their learning.

Suggested steps

1. You ask a question that *multiple students* are required to answer, but none of them can.
2. You let students know what the correct answer should be and tell them that they need to learn this within a set period (for example, by the next lesson), ensuring they have the necessary support resources.
3. You make a note to remind yourself to ask the question again. This might include the names of students who couldn't answer. If no one in the class can answer, you note that.
4. After this period has passed, you ask the question again, focusing on the students who couldn't answer it originally.

Example

In a music lesson...

Teacher   'Last lesson we were learning about different genres of music from the 1980s. Who would like to remind us what these were?'

The teacher pauses. Tumbleweed.

Teacher   'Would you be able to tell us what one of these was please... Audrey?'

Audrey   'I don't know.'

Teacher   'Okay. Well, if I said one of them began with an S, would that help?'

Specific input | Focused reflection | **Deliberate practice**

Audrey	'No.'
Teacher	'Okay. James, would you be able to help out?'
James	'No.'
Teacher	'Right. Well, if anyone thinks they know even just one, put up your hand.'

No hands go up.

Teacher 'Okay, well that's a shame. This was something we discussed in our last lesson. There were three different genres: synth pop, hip-hop and house music. Try to remember that two of them rhyme with one another and two of them start with the same letter. You have these written in your knowledge organisers. I would like you to do some active study so that you know these when I ask everyone to write these on show-me boards tomorrow.'

Notes

For this to be successful, you need to make sure students have access to resources that will allow them to learn the correct answer. This might be a textbook, their notes jotter or a knowledge organiser.

It would also be helpful to make sure students have been taught how to use *active study* strategies to help learn information, such as read-cover-write-check-correct or flash cards (as opposed to students rereading material, highlighting it or copying it out, which are less effective learning strategies).

Power up your questioning

Theme 5: Getting more students to learn from each other
– to enrich the learning experience for everyone

Overview

Common Pitfalls	Power-Up Prompts	Trusted Techniques
1. Students not being expected to listen to and learn from each other. 2. Students answering too quietly for others to hear. 3. Paraphrasing.	Students listen carefully to each other's answers so they can learn from these. ■ To what extent is this typically true? ■ What do you currently do to ensure this? ■ What could you do to make this *even better*?	Bounce Catch Chart It Say It Again, Louder Amplify

Common Pitfall 1: Students not being expected to listen to and learn from each other

When questioning is at its best, **whole-class teaching is effectively a discussion**. Students are listening to each other, and they comment on each other's answers. The teacher does this too. As a result, learning is *collaborative*.[82] There is energy, enthusiasm and active engagement.

However, collaborative learning through whole-class questioning is impossible to achieve if students don't appreciate that they are *expected* to listen to one another. It is the teacher's job to make this expectation clear, to explain why this is important and to create the conditions for this to happen. In other words, it is the teacher's job to *teach* students to listen to one another. Ultimately, we should be aiming to establish a listening culture in which students listen automatically.

Why isn't there a listening culture in every classroom?

The reason a listening culture doesn't exist in every classroom is because, in many, students have learned that when a teacher asks a question, one or more of the following will happen:

- Only students with their hand up will be chosen to answer.
- Only one student will be chosen to answer, so the odds of *them* being chosen are slim.
- Once someone has answered, no one else will be asked.

If any of these things are happening, it shouldn't be a surprise that many students believe that there is no requirement for them to always be listening. We can see this in the following examples.

---

[82] Sometimes, 'collaborative learning' is misunderstood to only mean 'group work'.

Specific input | Focused reflection | Deliberate practice

Example 1:

The teacher asks: 'What is a harmony?'

A student is chosen to answer and says: 'It's the sound created when two or more sounds of different pitch are played at the same time.' [This is correct.]

The teacher says, 'Good,' and moves on.

Example 2:

The teacher asks: 'What is a harmony?'

A student is chosen to answer and says: 'It's the sound created when two or more sounds are played at the same time.' [This is partially correct but is missing the key point about different pitches that was given in example 1.]

The teacher says, 'Nearly – but remember the different sounds have to be *different pitches*,' and moves on.

Dead-end questioning

Both of the above are examples of 'dead-end questioning'. Regardless of whether a student's answer is right or wrong, the questioning exchange finishes once an answer is given. There is no further interaction or collaboration with other students.

Now, contrast examples 1 and 2 with example 3.

Example 3:

The teacher asks: 'What is a harmony?'

Specific input | Focused reflection | Deliberate practice

A student, Laura, is chosen to answer and says: 'It's the sound created when two or more sounds of different pitch are played at the same time.' [This is correct.]

The teacher says, 'What do you think, Kelly? Is she right?'

Kelly says, 'I think so, yes.'

The teacher says, 'Okay, good. Which parts of the answer do you think are the most important to include?'

Kelly says, 'The bit about two or more.'

The teacher says, 'What do you think... Nicola?'

Nicola says, 'Yes, I agree.'

The teacher says, 'And are there any other parts that you think are important?'

Nicola says, 'The bit about different pitches.'

The teacher says, 'Good. So, Kelly has reminded us that the bit about two or more is important, and Nicola has reminded us that the bit about different pitches is important. Would anyone like to highlight anything else that they think is important?'

Some hands go up. The teacher waits. A few more hands go up. The teacher choses a student, Sharon, who has her hand up.

Sharon says, 'I think the bit about them being played at the same time is important.'

The teacher says, 'Good. So do I. That's three parts to the answer that we've highlighted as being important. Can you remind us what these three were please... Ahmed?'

Specific input | Focused reflection | Deliberate practice

In this example, the teacher has used the technique **Bounce** to encourage students to listen to, think about and respond to each other's answers. Rather than the teacher telling a student if an answer is right or wrong immediately, other students are first given the opportunity to comment. The teacher's role is to facilitate this.

Another useful technique is **Catch**. With this, a student answers a question, and another student is asked to repeat back what was said word for word. Again, this encourages students to listen to and learn from one another.

> **Pitfall Avoidance Principle**
> For (at least) every third targeted question, ask a collaborative follow-up question.

Chart It

One further thing that teachers can do to help students learn from each other is use the technique **Chart It**. With this, answers that students give to questions are written on the board for everyone to see and refer back to. In the busyness of lessons, it can be easy for students (and the teacher) to forget points that were made previously. Making a visual, written record helps prevent that.

Common Pitfall 2: Students answering too quietly for others to hear

Often when students answer questions during whole-class teaching, they speak too quietly for everyone to hear what they have said. Sometimes this is because they are shy and sometimes it is because they aren't confident in what they are saying. Regardless, if we believe it is important for the class to learn together – with and from one another – **we need to do something to help everyone hear the answers other students give**.

Specific input | Focused reflection | Deliberate practice

One of the things we can do is ask students to **Say It Again, Louder**. Alternatively, we can **Amplify** students' answers, whereby we repeat what was said word for word, loud enough for everyone to hear. The more we do these things, the more likely it is that students will come to learn that they are expected to answer loudly enough for everyone to hear, and the less of a need we will have for these techniques.

> **Pitfall Avoidance Principle**
>
> Take steps to ensure every student can hear the answer given by every other student.
>
> Question → Quiet answer → Teacher comments on answer and moves on
>
> Question → Quiet answer → **Teacher asks student to repeat their answer, but louder**
>
> Question → Quiet answer → **Teacher repeats answer word for word, but louder**

Common Pitfall 3: Paraphrasing

If we choose to repeat a student's answer to a question ourselves (to **Amplify**), the main pitfall to avoid is **paraphrasing**, whereby we correct words or phrases within the answer without drawing attention to the fact that we have done so. For example, in an art lesson, we might show students a painting and ask what kind it is. A student answers, 'A portrait,' and you say, 'That's right, it's a self-portrait.'

This is actually a very common thing for teachers to do. Sometimes they do it to be kind (they want students to be successful, and because they were nearly there with a correct answer, they 'polish it up' for them) and sometimes they do it because they're mindful of the time and they want to move on quickly. Either way, the effect on students' learning is unlikely to be a positive one.

If a teacher paraphrases, the change from the student's answer needs to be made crystal clear to everyone. In the art lesson example, this might involve the teacher saying something like:

- 'Nearly. Remember, because it was painted by the person themselves, it's a *self*-portrait.'
- 'Nearly. Remember, because it was painted by the person themselves, it's a…'

The second of these two options will probably be better for the student's learning because this requires them to do more of the cognitive work themselves. They have to tussle with long-term memory to retrieve the correct answer. This will almost always be more beneficial to their learning than if they are simply told the correct answer by the teacher. Retrieval strengthens memories and makes them less likely to be forgotten in a way that being shown or told things again does not.

Pitfall Avoidance Principle

Try not to paraphrase students' answers. If you do make changes, make this explicitly clear.

❌ Question → Incorrect answer → Teacher repeats with paraphrasing

✓ Question → Incorrect answer → **Teacher repeats back, word for word → Discussion of answer**

✓ Question → Incorrect answer → **Teacher corrects, making corrections explicitly clear**

Specific input | Focused reflection | Deliberate practice

Power-Up Prompts

Students listen carefully to each other's answers so they can learn from these.
1. To what extent is this typically true?
2. What do you currently do to ensure this?
3. What could you do to make this *even better*?

Deeper-Thinking Questions

Reflection/coaching questions for *before* a lesson:
1. What steps do you plan to take in this lesson to ensure students are listening carefully to each other's answers?
2. Are there particular Trusted Techniques you will be focusing on?
3. If so, what specific aspects of these techniques will you consciously be trying to do well?

Reflection/coaching questions for *after* a lesson:
1. To what extent do you feel your students listened carefully to each other's answers?
2. Can you give a specific example of when this happened especially well?
3. Were there particular Trusted Techniques you were using to help with this?
4. How successful do you think these were?
5. Is there anything you think you could have done to make these more successful?
6. Are there any other techniques you could use to make this even better?

Trusted Technique 1: Bounce

After a student has answered a question, you ask a different student to comment or build on the answer given. For example, you might say:

- 'Do you agree... [name student]?'
- 'What do you think about what he has just said... [name student]?'
- 'Who would like to comment on that?'
- 'Please could you build on what was just said... [name student].'

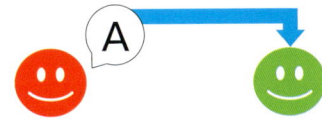

Why use it? (STAR: Spotlight, Thinking, Attention, Responding)

Bounce ensures that everyone is listening to all answers. By doing so, it helps establish a collaborative learning environment in which students understand they are expected to learn with and from one another, not just the teacher. Sometimes, students can pick up on things in other students' answers that the teacher might have missed.

This technique can also help students clarify their thinking. For example, if a student has commented on the answer given by another student, the student who gave the original answer might come back and say, 'No, that's not what I meant to say. What I meant to say was...'

Suggested steps

1. You ask a question and a student answers (correctly or incorrectly).
2. You ask *at least one* other student to comment or build on this answer.
3. You clarify the main teaching points from what has been said in the exchange.

Example

In an English lesson...

Teacher	'Can you give us an example of a simile, please… [pause] …Tessa?'
Tessa	'As light as a feather.'
Teacher	'Thanks, Tessa. Is she right… Adele?'
Adele	'Yes.'
Teacher	'Why is that?'
Adele	'Because a simile is when we use "like" or "as" in a sentence.'
Teacher	'What do you think about that… Jean?'
Jean	'I don't think that's quite right. I think the sentence has to be comparing things to be a simile.'
Teacher	'Okay, that's interesting. Can you comment on that, please… Samuel?'
Samuel	'Yeah, I think that's right. Because if I said "I like cows", that wouldn't be a simile.'
Teacher	'Good example. Okay, so back to you, Adele. Could you tell us what a simile is, please?'
Adele	'It's when we *compare things* using "like" or "as".'

Teacher	'That's better. Okay, can you give us a different example of a simile… Henry?'
Henry	'As cold as ice.'
Teacher	'Great. Okay, everyone, on your show-me boards, give me another example of a simile.'

Notes

Because the technique is likely to involve multiple exchanges, it is important that you take time to clarify and summarise the key points from these, or do something to check understanding, so students aren't left confused about what they should be learning.

Trusted Technique 2: Catch

After a student has answered a question, you ask a different student to repeat back what was said word for word.

Why use it? (STAR: Spotlight, Thinking, Attention, Responding)

Catch is useful for checking that students are paying attention. It can also give students multiple exposures to a particular answer, increasing the likelihood that the answer will be remembered.

Specific input | Focused reflection | **Deliberate practice**

Suggested steps

1. You ask a question and choose a student to answer.
2. The student answers.
3. You ask a *different student* to repeat the answer given.
4. If there are mistakes in this, you do something to make these clear. The same student is then expected to have another go at answering correctly.
5. [Optional.] You repeat steps 3 and 4 with other students.

Example

In a PE lesson...

Teacher 'Last lesson, we were learning about the four factors that can impact performance. Can you tell us what these were, please... [pause]... James?'

James 'Physical, mental, emotional and... social.'

Teacher 'That's super, James. You got all four. Robert, please tell us what James just said.'

Robert 'Social... physical... I'm not sure of the others.'

Teacher 'Well, James did just tell us. It's important you are listening. The two you said were correct. Remind us what the other two were, please... Lisa.'

Lisa 'Mental and emotional.'

Teacher 'Thanks. Right, Robert, another chance to give us all four, please.'

Robert 'Social, physical, mental and emotional.'

Specific input | Focused reflection | **Deliberate practice**

Teacher 'Well done. Campbell – your turn. Tell us what the four factors are that we need to remember, please.'

Campbell 'Physical, social, emotional and mental.'

Teacher 'Perfect. Everyone needs to know all four. I'm going to ask again later in the lesson, just to check everyone does.'

Notes

With Catch, we aren't necessarily trying to catch students out. It's human nature that attention can wander, and this technique is designed to help rein this in. If attention *has* wandered, the technique addresses this by giving students a second chance to hear or think about something that is important. We don't need to overdo any point we make to students about the importance of paying attention (unless this is a regular problem for them).

Trusted Technique 3: Chart It

Key words and phrases from a student's answer are written onto the board for everyone to see and refer back to.

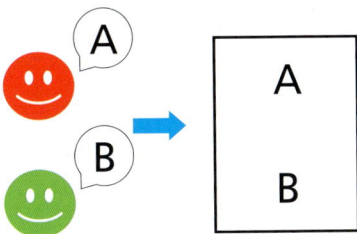

Specific input | Focused reflection | **Deliberate practice**

Why use it? (STAR: Spotlight, Thinking, Attention, Responding)

There is a limit to how much information students can hold in their working memories. This can be a particular problem when a class is learning new things with unfamiliar terminology or when multiple points are getting made during the course of whole-class discussion. Writing key words and phrases on the board leaves more space for thinking in working memory.

Sometimes, students can mishear or misinterpret the answers other students have given. For example, someone might say 'euthanasia', which someone else might hear as 'youth in Asia'. Writing what was said on the board helps avoid such misunderstandings.

Also, spelling matters. By writing key words and phrases on the board, students can see what these look like and how they are spelt.

Suggested steps

1. You ask a question, a student answers and you write key words or phrases from this on the board.
2. If appropriate, you draw students' attention to particular aspects of these, such as spelling.
3. You repeat steps 1 and 2 with answers from other students.
4. At appropriate points, you refer back to what is written on the board and encourage students to do the same.

Example

In a science lesson...

Teacher 'Today we are going to start a new topic on genetics. I'm wondering what you know about genetics already. Would anyone like to share what they know?'

Specific input | Focused reflection | **Deliberate practice**

The teacher pauses for 20 seconds, scanning the room and waiting for more and more hands to go up.

Teacher 'Maer, why don't you start us off.'

Maer 'Genetics is to do with the genes that we have in our bodies.'

Teacher 'Okay, that's a nice start. *Genes* is a key word.'

The teacher writes 'genes' onto the board.

Teacher 'So notice, everyone, that "genes" starts with a G, not a J. It's not like the spelling we use for clothes. Okay, who's next? Martin.'

Martin 'Genes are made up of DNA.'

Teacher 'That's good.'

The teacher writes 'DNA' on the board.

Teacher 'When we write "DNA", we should always use capital letters.'

The questions, answers and charting continue.

Notes

When writing key words and phrases on the board, take care to make your writing big enough for everyone to see (including at the back of the room) and to make it legible. This might seem obvious, but you'd be amazed at how many teachers don't do that.

Trusted Technique 4: Say It Again, Louder

A student's answer to a question is too quiet for everyone to hear, so the teacher asks them to say this again but with more volume.

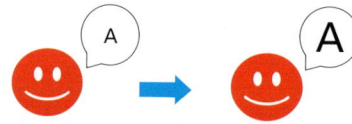

Why use it? (STAR: Spotlight, Thinking, Attention, Responding)

We are trying to establish a classroom culture in which everyone knows they are expected to listen to each other's answers. Clearly, this can only happen if students' answers are loud enough for everyone to hear.

Suggested steps

1. You ask a question that a student answers quietly.
2. You ask the student to repeat their answer loud enough for everyone to hear.
3. The student repeats their answer.
4. If it is now loud enough, you carry on. If it isn't, you ask the student for their answer to be *even louder* (taking care not to embarrass them).

Specific input | Focused reflection | **Deliberate practice**

Example

In a history lesson...

Teacher   'What were the key learning points from our last lesson on the Scottish witch trials... [pause] ... Louise?'

Louise   [Quietly.] 'We learned that they started to take place in the 1560s and that about 2500 people were executed.'

Teacher   'That's a good answer. Could you just repeat it so everyone can hear, please?'

Louise   [Louder.] 'We learned that they started to take place in the 1560s and that about 2500 people were executed.'

Teacher   'Thanks, Louise. Right... Robert, could you comment or build on that, please?'

The question–answer exchange continues.

Notes

Ultimately, this is a technique we are aiming to make redundant. We should be aiming create a culture in which every student *knows* that they are expected to answer loud enough for everyone to hear. The more we use the technique, the less need there should be for it.

Many students are naturally shy, which we should keep in mind when using this technique. This technique is about coaxing and encouraging louder answers, not pulling them out kicking and screaming. In the longer term, we hope the technique will help build students' confidence.

Sometimes, students will make changes to their original answer when asked to repeat it louder. If this happens, point out the change and ask the student which of the two they'd like to stick with.

Specific input | Focused reflection | **Deliberate practice**

Trusted Technique 5: Amplify

A student's answer to a question is too quiet for everyone to hear, so the teacher repeats back what they have said, word for word, without paraphrasing, so everyone can hear.

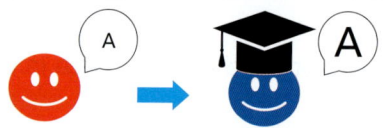

Why use it? (STAR: Spotlight, Thinking, Attention, Responding)

This technique helps support the development of a 'listening culture' in classrooms. Some students are very shy and struggle with speaking loud enough for everyone to hear. Ultimately, we want to build their confidence and get them to a point where they are happy to speak louder, but it can take time to get there. This technique addresses that.

Suggested steps

1. You ask a question and a student answers, but this is too quiet for everyone to hear.
2. You repeat the answer in a louder voice, word for word, without paraphrasing.

Example

In a business management lesson...

Teacher 'Let's recap what we should have learned about stakeholders to this point. Can I have one way in which an owner can influence a business, please... Oliver.'

Specific input | Focused reflection | **Deliberate practice**

Oliver	[Quietly.] 'They can withdraw equity.'
Teacher	'They can withdraw equity. What do you think… Kate? Is he right?' [The teacher has amplified the answer.]
Kate	'Yes, I think he is.'
Teacher	'Agreed. One of the things managers can do to influence a business is *withdraw equity*. Can you add anything to this, Kate?'
Kate	[Quietly.] 'They can also invest equity.'
Teacher	'That's a good answer. They can *invest equity* too.' [Again, the teacher has amplified the answer.]

Notes

As with **Say It Again, Louder**, this is a technique we are ultimately hoping to make redundant because we are trying to teach students to speak loud enough whenever they answer a question. As previously discussed, the main pitfall to avoid with this technique is the temptation to paraphrase, whereby we correct or improve students' answers without making this explicitly clear. If we do that, we risk students missing that there were mistakes in the original answer.

Specific input | Focused reflection | **Deliberate practice**

Power up your questioning

Theme 6: Making time to check understanding and review learning
– so you can adjust your teaching accordingly

Overview

Common Pitfalls	Power-Up Prompts	Trusted Techniques
1. Judging understanding (and learning) based on confidence rather than evidence. 2. Moving on before you have sufficient evidence of success. 3. Skipping opportunities to actively review short- and longer-term learning.	There is regular use of active review to check understanding and learning (short- and longer-term). ■ To what extent is this typically true? ■ What do you currently do to ensure this? ■ What could you do to make this *even better*?	Chunk It Quick Summary Success Criterion Check-in Exit Tickets Daily, Weekly & Monthly Review

Common Pitfall 1: Judging understanding (and learning) based on confidence rather than evidence

At one point or another, every teacher has probably asked, 'Does everyone understand?' and used the responses from a handful of students as a measure of how successfully they have taught something. Sometimes, students nod (or shake) their heads, there is a chorus of 'Yes!' (less often, 'No!'), we ask for thumbs-up (or -across or -down) or we use traffic-light cards. Other times, we ask the related question 'Does anyone have any questions?' and take the ensuing silence or chorus of 'no' to mean they've got it!

But of course, the problem with all of these things is that none of them tell us anything about what students have actually understood (or learned).[83] All they tell us is what students *believe* they have understood (or learned), which is very often different from the reality. We have asked for confidence measures and most students are likely to be *overconfident* in their responses.[84] They confuse something making sense, or being 'fresh in their minds', with understanding or learning it. Some students would have us believe they understand something simply because it's the easy thing to do, even though they don't.

Prove it!

The only way for teachers (and students) to know that something has *actually* been understood (or learned) is for students to engage in a task that requires them to prove it, using Trusted Techniques such as **Chunk It**, **Quick Summary**, **Success Criterion Check-In**, **Exits Tickets** and **Daily, Weekly & Monthly Review**. In other words, they have to produce evidence of understanding (or learning). Usually, this means they need to articulate it by verbalising their thinking or putting it in writing.[85]

---

83 *Understanding* can be thought of as a crucial step towards *learning*, but they are not the same thing.
84 Bjork, E.L. and Bjork, R.A. (2014) 'Making things hard on yourself, but in a good way.'
85 In subjects with practical components, this might require some form of performance.

For example, imagine a class has been reading the second chapter of *Watership Down*. At the end of the chapter, rather than ask the class to give a thumbs-up, thumbs-across or thumbs-down regarding how confident they feel about their understanding of something, the teacher could do one or more of the following:

1. Ask students to **Chat to a Partner**, summarising the key points in two minutes. After two minutes, ask students to swap roles. Students' ability to do this (or not) should give *them* evidence of what they actually understand. If the teacher listens in to conversations, they will get evidence of this too.
2. Ask a series of targeted questions that students are required to answer on **Show-Me Boards**.
3. Ask students to take five minutes to Empty Your Brain, writing the main points from the chapter in their jotter. As they do this, the teacher can move around the room looking at what is being written.

Pitfall Avoidance Principle

Rather than ask 'Does everyone understand?' or use other confidence measures, build regular 'prove it' tasks into lessons.

 'Does everyone understand?' → 'Yes' → Move on

 'Does anyone have any questions?' → 'No' → Move on

 Tasks that elicit *evidence* of understanding (or learning)

Common Pitfall 2: Moving on before you have sufficient evidence of success

One of the biggest challenges for teachers is knowing when it is best to move from one part of a lesson to another. For example, if you have asked students to answer a question on **Show-Me Boards** and half the class get this correct and half the class don't, should you move on to a more challenging question or the next part of the lesson, or should you stick to where you are and address this?

The answer relies on striking a sensible balance between two overarching principles:

1. Ultimately, our aim is for *every* student to learn *everything* set out in the curriculum (however aspirational that might be).
2. Realistically, different students are going to learn at different rates. At some point, we do have to move on as a class, even though we know some students haven't yet grasped what we are teaching.

The second principle doesn't mean that we believe it is okay to leave any student behind – of course it isn't. Rather, it means that with the best interests of everyone in mind, there does come a point when things need to move forward. **The students who 'aren't there yet' will get teacher support at a later point in the lesson**. For example, there might be *temporary grouping* and *reteaching* while the rest of the class engage with consolidation or extension activity. Or there might be *out-of-class support*.

The 80% Success Rule

The 80% Success Rule can be used by teachers to decide when best to move on in a lesson: move on to the next stage once you have evidence of success from *at least* 80% of the class. In a class of 20 students, this would mean from *at least* 16 students; in a class of 30, it would mean from *at least* 24. Moving on before this probably leaves too many students behind.

Specific input | Focused reflection | Deliberate practice

Pitfall Avoidance Principle

Look for evidence of success from at least 80% of the class before moving on.

 Question → Less than 80% success → Move on

 Question → **At least 80% success** → Move on

 Question → Less than 80% success → **Reteach and recheck** → **At least 80% success** → Move on

Common Pitfall 3: Skipping opportunities to actively review short- and longer-term learning

Checking students' understanding in the moment is important. However, equally important is checking this again at *multiple points* in future. The reason is because, over time, learning fades and understanding changes.[86] Just because you had evidence that students understood (or appeared to have learned) something as it was being taught, it doesn't mean they will still understand (or remember) this a few days later. Evidence of short-term learning (that is *performance* in the moment) is no guarantee of longer-term learning.

To appreciate this, imagine you are teaching a lesson on the architecture of the Eiffel Tower. At the end of this, you ask students to complete **Exit Tickets** that require them to answer three questions designed

---

86 As discussed in the 'Learning and how it happens' section.

to check knowledge and understanding (short-term learning). You review these after the lesson and, to your delight, discover that all students have answered every question correctly. However, to your dismay, when you kick-off the next lesson three days later with a review of content from the previous lesson, you discover that more than half the class can no longer answer the same questions. They *did* understand, but now they don't.

Regular active revisits are essential

The fact that learning *will* fade, no matter how good the teaching was originally, means it is essential for teachers to plan regular revisits of previously taught content. At their most effective, these revisits will be active (requiring retrieval) rather than passive (students being shown or told things again).[87] They will also be built around short- (within the same lesson), medium- (within a few days) and long-term (within a few weeks or months) review cycles:[88]

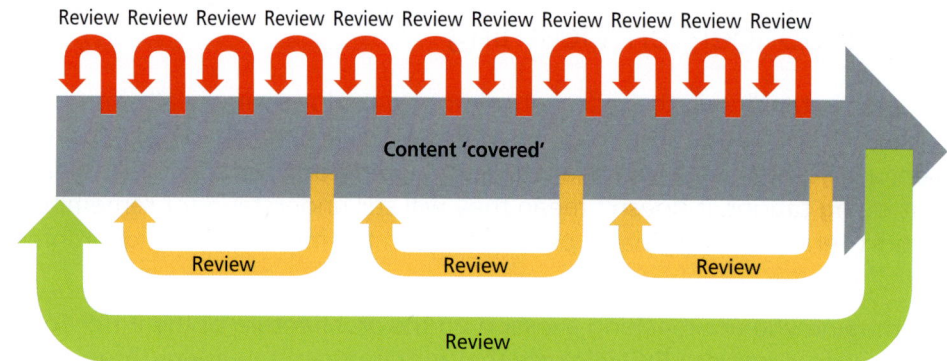

---

87 So that they utilise the testing effect as discussed in the 'Learning and how it happens' section.
88 So that they utilise the forgetting effect as discussed in the 'Learning and how it happens' section.

Use of such cycles can help teachers to find out where students *actually* are in their learning, rather than where they *hope* they are. Great teaching isn't about starting where we want to and ploughing on regardless. It is about eliciting rigorous evidence of where students are in their learning and responding accordingly.

Trusted Techniques that can help with short-cycle review include **Chunk It**, **Quick Summary**, **Success Criterion Check-in** and **Exit Tickets**.

Pitfall Avoidance Principle

Gather evidence that something has been understood, allow some time to pass, then ask students questions that require retrieval of the same material.

A Trusted Technique that can help with medium- and long-cycle review is **Daily, Weekly & Monthly Review**.[89] Homework programmes that focus on independent practice tasks covering recent and less-recent material can also help.[90]

Pitfall Avoidance Principle

Start lessons with an active review of prior learning.

 Beginning lessons with a 'starter' that does little more than keep students busy

 Beginning lessons with a short, active review of prior learning, including content related to this lesson

---

89 Rosenshine, B. (2012) 'Principles of instruction.'
90 These needn't create more work for the teacher. More often than not, they can be marked with students during lesson time.

Pitfall Avoidance Principle

Finish each week and month with an active review of curriculum content, including both recent and less-recently covered material.

Pitfall Avoidance Principle

Use your homework programme to support learning via spaced retrieval of both recent and less recent material.

 Homework programmes that focus *only* on self-study or recently covered content

 Homework programmes that build in active review of recently and less-recently taught content

Power-Up Prompts

There is regular use of active review to check understanding and learning (short- and longer-term).

1. To what extent is this typically true?
2. What do you currently do to ensure this?
3. What could you do to make this *even better*?

Specific input | **Focused reflection** | Deliberate practice

Deeper-Thinking Questions

Reflection/coaching questions for *before* a lesson:
1 At what points in the lesson do you plan to check understanding?
2 How do you plan to do that?
3 What short- and longer-term learning do you plan to explore in Daily Review?
4 Why have you decided to focus on the areas you have chosen?
5 What specific prior knowledge do you need to check before teaching new content in this lesson?
6 How do you plan to do that?

Reflection/coaching questions for *after* a lesson:
1 Do you think you did enough to check understanding at key points in the lesson?
2 Do you believe you got sufficient evidence of everyone's understanding at key points in the lesson?
3 Was there anything you could have done to improve your checks for understanding?
4 How effectively do you feel you used Daily Review in this lesson?
5 Is there particular content you feel needs to be revisited in a future Daily, Weekly & Monthly Review or in homework?

Specific input | **Focused reflection** | Deliberate practice

Trusted Technique 1: Chunk It

Part-way through or at the end of a period of teacher exposition, the teacher pauses to actively review the content covered to that point, using preplanned closed questions.

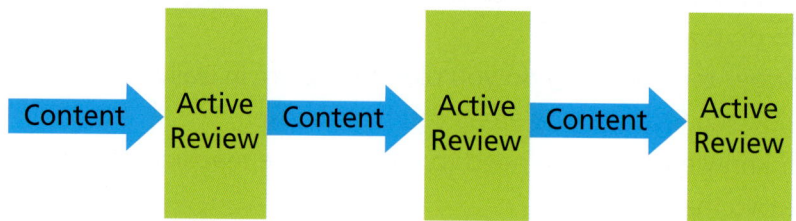

Why use it? (STAR: Spotlight, Thinking, Attention, Responding)

This technique helps you gauge the size of the current teaching–learning gap. Based on what you discover, you can address this either in the moment or at some point in future.

By generating *evidence* of their understanding, students should have a better idea of what they have actually understood, as opposed to what they believe they did.

This technique requires retrieval, which strengthens memory, and can break up periods of teacher exposition, helping hold students' attention and interest.

Suggested steps

1. As part of your planning, you determine the points in a lesson that would lend themselves best to an active review. As a rule of thumb, aim for at least every 15 minutes.
2. You plan a question, or short series of questions, that should be good for active review at each of these planned points.

Specific input | Focused reflection | **Deliberate practice**

3   When you reach each planned point, you ask *all students* to engage with each question. For example, you might use **Show-Me Boards** or **Chat to a Partner**.
4   [Optional.] As students are engaging, you circulate the room, either listening in to discussions or looking at what students are writing. You make mental or physical notes (perhaps in a notepad).
5   Invite students to share responses to each question with the rest of the class.
6   Give feedback and summarise the key points you want students to learn.
7   If necessary, reteach anything that you feel has been poorly understood.

Example

In a history lesson as part of a series about conflict and tension between the East and the West, 1945–1972…

The teacher has been delivering an interactive presentation to the class. Fifteen minutes in, a slide appears with the heading 'Checkpoint time' and three preplanned questions:

1   Which two countries were regarded as the global 'superpowers' at this time?
2   Which of these two was communist and which was capitalist?
3   What do the terms 'communist' and 'capitalist' mean?

The teacher tells the class that they want everyone to answer the first question on **Show-Me Boards**. On seeing students' answers, they give whole-class feedback and make the correct answers clear. They do the same with the second question. For the third question, knowing it is more complex and demanding, the teacher asks students to take one minute to **Chat to a Partner**. After this, they use **Cold Call** to find out what a selection of students were thinking, then they give whole-class feedback, which includes making the answers clear.

Specific input | Focused reflection | **Deliberate practice**

Notes

Obviously, we have a curriculum to cover, so there are limits to how much time we can spend on **Chunk It**. However, if we don't make at least *some* time for this, we risk leaving students behind without realising and creating unnecessarily large gaps between what we are trying to teach and what students are actually learning.

Usually, this technique involves the teacher in some shape or form. However, even if there were no teacher involvement, it should still have value. For example, if students are asked to explain their understanding to a partner and they discover they can't do this properly, there is formative value *for them*. That said, it is usually better if the teacher knows what students are saying or writing as well.

Trusted Technique 2: Quick Summary

Part-way through or at the end of a period of teacher exposition, the teacher pauses to actively review the content covered to that point, using an open, reflective task.

Specific input | Focused reflection | **Deliberate practice**

Why use it? (STAR: Spotlight, Thinking, Attention, Responding)

This technique helps you gauge the size of the current teaching–learning gap. Based on what you discover, you can address this either in the moment or at some point in future.

By generating evidence of their understanding, students should have a better idea of what they have actually understood, as opposed to what they believe they did.

This technique requires retrieval, which strengthens memory and can break up periods of teacher exposition, helping hold students' attention and interest.

Suggested steps

1 As part of your planning, you determine the points in a lesson that would lend themselves best to an active review. As a rule of thumb, aim for at least every 15 minutes.

2 When you reach each planned point, you ask all students to engage with an open, reflective task, such as:
   - Write down everything you have understood from the last 15 minutes.
   - Chat to a partner about what you think are the key learning points from what we have just discussed.

3 [Optional.] As students are engaging, you circulate the room, either listening to discussions or looking at what students are writing. You make mental or physical notes (perhaps in a notepad).

4 Invite students to share responses to each question with the rest of the class.

5 Give feedback and summarise the key points you want students to learn.

6 If necessary, reteach anything that you feel has been poorly understood.

Specific input | Focused reflection | **Deliberate practice**

Example

In a modern studies lesson...

The teacher has been talking to the class about alternative punishments to prison using an interactive PowerPoint presentation. Fifteen minutes into the presentation (which is planned to last for 30 minutes), a slide appears that reads 'Quick summary'.

Teacher 'I would like everyone to take five minutes and write down what you think are the key points we have covered so far in your jotter.'

The teacher circulates the room, looking at jotters as they move around. They have a notebook with them, which they use to jot down key things they are seeing. After five minutes, they re-address the class.

Teacher 'Everyone stop there, thank you. Right, so I saw a few interesting things. Firstly, I saw many of you writing [this]. Well done. That's a very important point. However, I saw a few of you writing [this]. Be careful with that – that's not quite right. What should we have been writing, please… Tom?'

Tom gives a correct answer.

Teacher 'Good. Okay, who would like to share some other points that they wrote down?'

Hands go up and the teacher chooses different students to answer, giving feedback on what is said each time.

Notes

This technique is essentially a variation on **Chunk It**, with a more 'open' focus to the reflective task. As discussed as part of 'Theme 2: Asking better questions', open tasks of this kind will often uncover learning gaps and misunderstandings that otherwise would have remained hidden, had the teacher not made time to explore this.

As students attempt to write or articulate their thinking, they will tend to refine this, which is good for their learning and to discover things that they don't understand that they thought they did. As we have said, just because content is familiar (because it has been covered recently), it doesn't mean it has been understood.

Trusted Technique 3: Success Criterion Check-In

This technique can be used in lessons that have multiple 'I can...' success criteria. At planned points in the lesson, students are reminded of the success criteria and asked to complete a short task that checks short-term learning relating to one of these.

```
Criterion 1     Prove it

Criterion 2

Criterion 3
```

Why use it? (STAR: Spotlight, Thinking, Attention, Responding)

Revisiting success criteria helps to remind students (and the teacher) what they are trying to achieve in a lesson.

Students' performance in the **Success Criterion Check-In** task should help the teacher to gauge the size of the teaching–learning gap, so they can respond accordingly. By generating evidence, students should have a better idea of what they actually know and can do, as opposed to what they believe to be true.

This technique requires retrieval, which strengthens memory, and can break up periods of teacher exposition, helping hold students' attention and interest.

Suggested steps

1 You share 'I can…' success criteria with students towards the start of a lesson.
2 Following a period of teaching, you pause and revisit these criteria, drawing students' attention to the criterion that relates directly to what has just been covered.
3 You ask students a question (or questions) designed to generate evidence of short-term learning relating to this criterion.
4 You respond accordingly before teaching continues.
5 You repeat steps two to four at planned points later in the lesson.

Example

In a history lesson that has two success criteria:
1 *I can give at least two reasons why the Greeks created myths and legends.*
2 *I can outline at least three key events in the story of Atlantis.*

The teacher shares the success criteria with students towards the start of the lesson. They then move into an interactive PowerPoint presentation. Midway through this, a slide appears with the heading 'Success criterion check-in'. The first criterion is highlighted, and the teacher asks students to use **Show-Me Boards** to prove they can do this.

Specific input | Focused reflection | **Deliberate practice**

Looking at boards, the teacher can see that most students can, but a few can't. The teacher summarises correct answers and makes it clear that this criterion is going to be revisited again at the end of the lesson and that they will be looking for *all students* to be able to meet it.

In the final five minutes of the lesson, the teacher again revisits the success criteria with students. They ask two questions, each relating to a different criterion. Students are asked to write answers on Show-Me Boards, which the teacher looks at. They use what they are seeing to guide their planning for the next lesson.

Notes

It can be helpful to think of success criteria as three different types:

1 'I can...' statements
2 Key features
3 Exemplars.

The type that is most appropriate will depend on what is being taught. This technique is specific to the first type.

Specific input | Focused reflection | **Deliberate practice**

Trusted Technique 4: Exit Tickets

In the final few minutes of a lesson, the teacher asks students to answer a question or a short set of questions designed to generate evidence of their short-term learning from the lesson. They review these ahead of the next lesson, adapting their lesson planning accordingly.

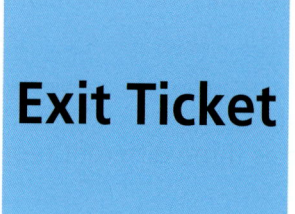

Why use it? (STAR: Spotlight, Thinking, Attention, Responding)

Students' answers in **Exit Tickets** should help you to gauge the size of the teaching–learning gap so you can respond to this in future lesson planning. By generating evidence, students should develop a better idea of what they actually know and can do, as opposed to what they believe to be true.

This technique requires retrieval, which strengthens memory.

Suggested steps

1. You pause the lesson a few minutes before it is due to end.
2. You ask students to write their responses to one or more questions on a piece of loose-leaf paper or a Post-it note. It is likely that most of these questions will have been planned ahead of the lesson, though you might choose to ask something in the moment based on information you gathered during the lesson.

Specific input | Focused reflection | **Deliberate practice**

3 Once students have finished, you collect their responses.

4 You review these ahead of the next lesson, making mental or written notes about points of interest, such as common mistakes or misconceptions. (There is no need to mark the tickets, though of course you can if you wish.)

5 You plan the next lesson with student responses to Exit Tickets in mind. For example, you might decide to begin the lesson by revisiting the tickets with students. Or you might decide to reteach particular content or to give students more practice at something.

Example

In a maths lesson on rounding numbers, students are asked the following Exit Ticket questions...

1 Round 246 to the nearest 5.
2 Round 246 to the nearest 10.
3 Round 246 to the nearest 100.

On reviewing these after the lesson, the teacher discovers that everyone bar one student got the first question correct, 20 out of 25 students got the second question correct, but only half the class got the third question correct. At the start of the next lesson, they go over the correct answers with students, briefly reteaching particular points. In the Exit Ticket task for this lesson, students are asked three similar questions to gauge how their understanding has developed:

1 Round 636 to the nearest 5.
2 Round 636 to the nearest 10.
3 Round 636 to the nearest 100.

Specific input | Focused reflection | **Deliberate practice**

Notes

The biggest pitfall teachers fall into with Exit Tickets (and plenaries in general) is not allowing enough time for them. They keep going and going with the lesson and, before they know it, there is only one minute to go. The bell sounds almost as soon as the Exit Ticket task has started, so students rush it or abandon it altogether. Either way, it means the Exit Ticket isn't taken seriously and, as a result, it offers little formative value to the teacher. So, the key point is **keep an eye on the clock** and, if you need to, set an alarm to remind you to start the Exit Ticket task.

There is no harm in asking an Exit Ticket question that has already been asked earlier in the lesson. In fact, there is often a lot of value in doing that. For example, if 20 minutes into the lesson you had asked the class to spell the words 'unnecessary', 'superficially' and 'obstreperous', and only a handful of students got all three correct, there would probably be great value in asking this question again in an Exit Ticket (assuming there had been corrective feedback). If any student complains they got all three correct the first time, you just need to tell them that you want to double check it wasn't a fluke.

Remember that Exit Tickets evidence *short-term learning*, not longer-term learning. Getting evidence that students know or understand something (or don't) by the end of a lesson can be important, but don't fall into the trap of believing that the 'learning' will still be there in future. This is where **Daily, Weekly & Monthly Review** can help (see the next Trusted Technique).

Trusted Technique 5: Daily, Weekly & Monthly Review

At some point during a lesson (usually towards the start for Daily Review), students are asked preplanned knowledge retrieval questions (closed or open). In the case of Daily Review, this includes at least one question that relates to the content of the lesson at hand.

Why use it? (STAR: Spotlight, Thinking, Attention, Responding)

Daily, Weekly & Monthly Review utilises both the testing effect[91] and the forgetting effect,[92] strengthening memory. Such reviews also help you to gauge the size of the teaching–learning gap as it currently is, as opposed to how it was in a previous lesson. In other words, these reviews generate evidence of how much content has been remembered or forgotten.

By asking students questions that relate to the content of the lesson at hand (in Daily Review), *schema activation* means students' long-term memories should become 'stickier', helping new knowledge to be remembered.[93]

---

91 Retrieval strengthens memory.
92 The more difficult a memory is to retrieve, the greater the impact of the testing effect.
93 As discussed in the 'Learning and how it happens' section.

Suggested steps

1. You preplan a set of questions designed to get students to retrieve previously covered knowledge. In the case of Daily Review, this includes knowledge that relates to the content of today's lesson.
2. You ring-fence time in your lesson plan for students to engage with these questions.
3. You ask the questions in a way that requires *every student* to think about *every question*.
4. You take steps to find out about the thinking of as many students as you can. For example, you might use **Show-Me Boards**.
5. You make notes (mental or physical) of any significant errors so that you can respond to these at a future point.

Example

Daily Review: At the start of a physics lesson about heat transfer (specifically, convection), three questions appear on the screen.

1. True or false: we measure heat in degrees Celsius. If false, correct the statement.
2. Explain why the following sentence is wrong: the sea, with a temperature of 15°C, has less heat in it than a bowl of soup, with a temperature of 80°C.
3. Write as many differences between *temperature* and *heat* as you can.

The teacher tells students they have four minutes to write answers in their jotter under the heading 'Daily Review'. As students are answering, the teacher circulates the room to get a feel for what students are writing for each question.

After four minutes, the teacher stops the class and goes over answers. Although there isn't time on this occasion to find out what every student has written for every question, the Daily Review activity has been successful at activating relevant schema, utilising the testing effect and the forgetting effect, helping the teacher to get a feel for where students are in their learning, and giving students the opportunity to hear the correct answer to each question from the teacher. If the Daily Review hadn't taken place, none of this would have happened.

Weekly or Monthly Review: The teacher stops the class 10 minutes before the end of the lesson, telling students that it is time for Weekly (or Monthly) Review. A series of questions appear on a PowerPoint slide, one at a time. Some of these are 'closed' and some are 'open'. When a question appears, students are given an appropriate amount of time to write answers on **Show-Me Boards**, which they hold up for the teacher to see. Based on this, the teacher gives both individual and whole-class feedback. They make a note of common mistakes and questions that students have particular difficulty with. At the start of the next lesson, they plan to reteach some of this material.

Notes

The underpinning principles of Daily Review apply to Weekly and Monthly Review as well. The only significant differences are that Weekly and Monthly Review will likely cover more content and include a greater focus on less-recently taught material. For example, there might be questions relating to knowledge that was first taught six months ago.

As illustrated in the example, **Daily, Weekly & Monthly Review** needn't take the form of a quiz (though sometimes there is value in that approach). In other words, reviews of this kind can be used to do more than get students to recall surface knowledge (such as facts). By designing questions carefully, Daily, Weekly & Monthly Review can be used to check *deeper understanding* as well.

If you discover a significant number of students have answered a particular question incorrectly, you should make a note of this and include the same question in a future Daily, Weekly & Monthly Review or in homework.

As in any activity, it is important that your expectations for how Daily, Weekly & Monthly Review is carried out are made clear to students. If you want them to complete the task individually, they shouldn't be allowed to talk and there should be silence in the room. If you want students to talk about each question rather than write answers – for example, by using **Chat to a Partner** – you should make that clear too.

Teachers often worry about how much time Daily, Weekly & Monthly Review 'takes up', fixating on how much content is left to get through. However, as previously discussed, effective teaching isn't about getting through content – it is about students *learning* this. To ensure our teaching has been effective, we really do need to make time for Daily, Weekly & Monthly Review. Otherwise, we're just ploughing on regardless of what has been understood and learned previously. In the long-term, this is only going to lead to problems. Daily Review only requires a few minutes per lesson. Weekly Review needn't take much more than 5–10 minutes per week. Covering more content, Monthly Review will probably take a bit longer, but 10–15 minutes is likely to be sufficient. If we're honest with ourselves, the relatively short amount of time spent on these activities is likely to more than justify their inclusion.

Summary and further support resources

Summary of how to use this book

You might recall that, towards the start of *Power Up Your Questioning*, we discussed the following model for professional learning:

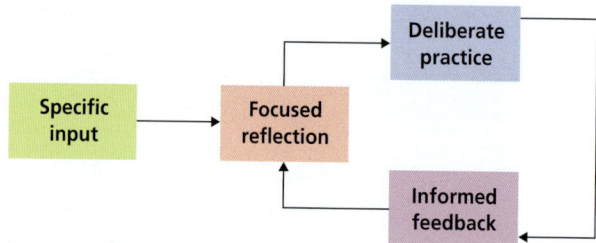

Linking the sections of this book to this model, we said that:
- The **Common Pitfalls** offer **specific input**.
- The **Power-Up Prompts** and **Deeper-Thinking Questions** support **focused reflection**.
- The **Trusted Techniques** are included to guide your **deliberate practice**.

We said that the only thing this book can't provide is a trusted colleague to offer **informed feedback** on your practice (so it's down to you or your school to set this up).

To get the most from this book, it was recommended that you follow 10 sequential steps:

1	Pick a theme...	...from one of the six explored.
2	Read...	...the **Common Pitfalls** relating to this theme.
3	Reflect...	...on your current practice using the **Power-Up Prompts** and **Deeper-Thinking Questions** to help guide your reflection.

4	Commit…	…to developing a specific aspect of your practice over the next 2-4 weeks, choosing one or more **Trusted Techniques** to focus on.[94]
5	Practise…	…this aspect in a deliberate way in every lesson over this period.
6	Revisit…	…the relevant sections of the book periodically to make sure you are on the right track.
7	Invite a colleague…	…to observe the aspect of practice you are working on at least once during the 2-4-week period. They don't have to observe a whole lesson – just a part relating to what you are working on.
8	Meet your colleague…	…to discuss their thoughts and suggestions. Use the **Common Pitfalls**, **Power-Up Prompts**, **Deeper-Thinking Questions** and/or **Trusted Techniques** sections to guide your discussion (choose the one you find the most useful).
9	Review…	…your progress and decide whether you have made sufficient improvements at the end of the 2-4-week period. ■ If you haven't, continue developing the aspect of practice you are currently working on. ■ If you have…
10	Choose another…	…aspect of practice to focus on. This might be from the same theme or a different one.

We said that steps 1–6 and 9–10 can be followed individually without the need to work with a colleague. Steps 7–8 focus on **pedagogical coaching** and require a colleague to work with.

We also said that while you will get a lot from the book on your own, you will get a lot more if you work with a colleague to follow steps 7 and 8 together using the pedagogical coaching approach outlined. This book finishes with two short, supplementary sections to support pedagogical coaching conversations:

- SURF: a framework to support pedagogical coaching conversations.
- Pedagogical coaching conversation examples.

---

[94] We said that not all techniques will work well on the first or second attempt. If you find that's the case, resist any temptation to give up. Many of the techniques take time and practice to master, and for students to get used to. Keep practising and revisit the details of the techniques in this book if you need to.

SURF: a framework to support pedagogical coaching conversations

If you are taking the role of a pedagogical coach, the most important point to keep in mind is that coaching conversations should feel *useful* to the teacher you are coaching. To ensure this, it is recommended you follow the **SURF** principles:

S	U	R	F
Specific – keep the conversation focused on particular aspects of teaching practice. Use of the **Common Pitfalls**, **Power-Up Prompts**, **Deeper-Thinking Questions** and/or **Trusted Techniques** should help with that.	**U**nderstood – make sure the teacher you are coaching really understands the key points and suggestions you are making. Questions such as 'Can you summarise the key points?' can be useful.	**R**esearch-informed – try to avoid falling into the trap of offering personal opinions and phrases such as 'I'm not sure I would do it like that.' Instead, focus on key evidence-informed messages, as discussed in the **Common Pitfalls** and **Trusted Techniques** sections.	**F**ollowed-up – finish meetings by agreeing a date and time for: 1 The next lesson you will observe 2 The next meeting to discuss what you saw in the lesson.

Pedagogical coaching conversation examples

Two examples of pedagogical coaching conversations are outlined below to help you get a feel for the format these might take and for how SURF principles can play out in practice. As you will hopefully appreciate, such conversations need only be 5–10 minutes long.

Example 1: first meeting (before a lesson is observed)

Both the teacher and the coach have a copy of this book with them for reference.

Coach   'Which element of practice are you focusing on developing?'

Teacher   'Questioning.'

Coach   'Have you had a chance to think about the **Power-Up Prompts** that relate to this?'

Teacher   'Yes. Thinking about the first one (*teacher exposition is infused with frequent questioning*), I think I am pretty good at asking lots of questions in lessons. However, I don't think I ask enough follow-up questions to explore students' thinking or to get students to comment on each other's answers.'

Coach   'Okay, that's interesting. So, which **Power-Up Prompts** do you think link closest to those areas?'

Teacher   'There are probably two: *questioning is used to develop both surface knowledge and deeper understanding* and *students listen carefully to each other's answers so they can learn from these*.'

Coach   'Great. It's probably best to focus on these one at a time. Do you have a preference as to which you start with?'

Summary and further support resources

Teacher 'I think we should start with the one about questioning being used to explore both surface knowledge and deeper understanding. I think that's probably the most important of the two for me at the moment.'

Coach 'Okay, that's good. So, is there a particular **Trusted Technique** you think would be worth practising to help you with that?'

Teacher 'I think "Drill Down" would be a good one.'

Coach 'And what is your understanding of that technique?'

Teacher 'As much as I can, I should be trying to follow-up an initial question with ones such as "Why do you think that?" or "Could you tell us a bit more about that?"'

Coach 'Yes, that's it. Open questions like that can be really useful. But if we go back to what the book says about this technique, I think closed questions can sometimes be useful too.'

The teacher and coach look at the relevant section in the book.

Teacher 'Yes, I see what you mean. It talks about using things like comparisons to explore deeper understanding. I think I could be doing that more often.'

Coach 'Okay, so we're agreeing that you're going to focus on developing the Drill Down technique to explore deeper understanding more. When would you like me to come into a lesson to watch that in action?'

Teacher 'I'd like two weeks to practise the technique with different classes. How about Monday 11th March at 11am?'

Coach 'Great. I'll look forward to joining you then.'

Example 2: second meeting (the day after the observed lesson)

Both the teacher and the coach have a copy of this book with them for reference.

Coach 'Thanks so much for having me in your lesson yesterday. I really enjoyed being there.'

Teacher 'It was great to have you. Hopefully you could see some examples of how I was using the Drill Down technique.'

Coach 'I definitely could. For example, I saw you use it during Daily Review in the first five minutes of the lesson.'

Teacher 'Yes. Every student had answered each of the three questions on Show-Me Boards, but I was able to use Drill Down to find out more about what students were thinking.'

Coach 'And was that useful?'

Teacher 'Absolutely. For example, I discovered that Derek had written the correct answer to the first question, but he'd arrived at it for the wrong reason. There was a misconception there that I would have missed otherwise.'

Coach 'And do you think you used Drill Down enough during this part of the lesson?'

Teacher 'To be honest, I think I could have used it a bit more. I asked three students why they had answered as they had for the first question, but I didn't use the technique for the second and third question. It would probably have been better if I had.'

Coach 'I wouldn't disagree. However, you obviously need to balance this against everything else you are hoping to do in the lesson.'

Teacher 'True. But I think it could have been manageable.'

Coach 'Fair enough. Maybe that's something to keep practising.'

Teacher	'Yes, definitely.'
Coach	'And I think in our last meeting you said you were going to start trying to use comparisons more in questioning. How is that going?'
Teacher	'Whenever I use comparisons, I'm definitely getting a lot more information about why students are thinking the way they are. However, if I'm being honest, I don't think I'm using them enough.'
Coach	'Why do you think you're not using them more?'
Teacher	'Probably because I'm not spending enough time planning questions like that in advance of lessons. I need to get better at that.'
Coach	'Okay, so shall we say that over the next two weeks you will practise using Drill Down *even more* than you have been, and you will practise planning more comparison questions?'
Teacher	'Yes, that's exactly it.'
Coach	'Great. Let's agree a date and time for the next lesson for me to watch.'

Afterword: power up in every lesson, every week

Power Up Your Questioning is a handbook that is designed to help you develop your teaching practice in *every lesson* you teach. With each passing week, you should feel like you are an *even better* teacher than you were before. As a member of the 'transforming lives' business, this is incredibly important. The more you learn and develop as a teacher, the more your students will learn and achieve, and the more satisfaction you'll get from your job. Everyone wins.

Beyond supporting the development of your questioning practice, hopefully this book sparks an interest in developing *students'* questioning practice as well. As catalysts for learning, the principles of asking more questions and better questions apply as much to them as they do to you.[95] The more questions students ask, and the better these are, the more learning is likely to happen. This is a great example of 'student-led learning' in action.

Keep powering up!

---

95 As suggested to me by John Hattie.

References

Ausubel, D., Novak, J. and Hanesian, H. (1978) *Educational Psychology: A Cognitive View* (2nd edition). New York, NY: Holt, Rinehart & Winston.

Barton, C. (2018) *How I Wish I'd Taught Maths*. Woodbridge: John Catt Educational.

Bjork, E.L. and Bjork, R.A. (2014) 'Making things hard on yourself, but in a good way: Creating desirable difficulties to enhance learning.' In Gernsbacher, M.A. and Pomerantz, J.R. (eds.) *Psychology and the Real World: Essays Illustrating Fundamental Contributions to Society* (2nd edition). New York, NY: Worth, pp. 59–68.

Brown, P.C., Roediger III, H.L. and McDaniel, M.A. (2014) *Make It Stick: The Science of Successful Learning*. Cambridge, MA: Harvard University Press.

Christodoulou, D. (2016) *Making Good Progress?: The Future of Assessment for Learning*. Oxford: Oxford University Press.

Coe, R., Rauch, C.J., Kime, S. and Singleton, D. (2020) *Great Teaching Toolkit: Evidence Review*. Evidence Based Education.

Enser, Z. and Enser, M. (2020) *Fiorella & Mayer's Generative Learning in Action*. Woodbridge: John Catt Educational.

Hattie, J. (2012) *Visible Learning for Teachers: Maximizing Impact on Learning*. New York, NY: Routledge.

Hendrick, C. and Macpherson, R. (2017) *What Does This Look Like in the Classroom? Bridging the Gap Between Research and Practice*. Woodbridge: John Catt Educational.

Hirsch, E.D. (2016) *Why Knowledge Matters: Rescuing Our Children from Failed Educational Theories*. Cambridge, MA: Harvard Education Press.

Kirschner, P.A. and Hendrick, C. (2020) *How Learning Happens: Seminal Works in Educational Psychology and What They Mean in Practice*. Oxon: Routledge.

Kirschner, P.A., Sweller, J. and Clark, R.E. (2010) 'Why minimal guidance during instruction does not work: An analysis of the failure of constructivist, discovery, problem-based, experiential, and inquiry-based teaching.' *Educational Psychologist*, 41(2): pp. 75–86.

Lemov, D. (2021) *Teach Like a Champion 3.0: 63 Techniques that Put Students on the Path to College*. San Francisco, CA: Jossey-Bass.

Mccrea, P. (2017) *Memorable Teaching: Leveraging Memory to Build Deep and Durable Learning in the Classroom*. CreateSpace Independent Publishing Platform.

McGill, R. M. (2011) *Pose, pause, pounce, bounce!* Available at: www.teachertoolkit.co.uk/2011/11/04/pose-pause-bounce-pounce/

Naylor, S. and Keogh, B. (2000) *Concept Cartoons in Science Education*. Cheshire: Millgate House Publishers.

Naylor, S., Keogh, B. and Goldsworthy, A. (2004) *Active Assessment: Thinking, Learning and Assessment in Science*. London: David Fulton.

Nuthall, G. (2007) *The Hidden Lives of Learners*. Wellington: NZCER Press.

Robertson, B. (2020) *The Teaching Delusion*. Woodbridge: John Catt Educational.

Rosenshine, B. (2012) 'Principles of instruction: Research-based strategies that all teachers should know.' *American Educator*, 36(1): pp. 12–19.

Shrestha, P. (2017) *Ebbinghaus Forgetting Curve*. Available at: www.psychestudy.com/cognitive/memory/ebbinghaus-forgetting-curve

Weinstein, Y. and Sumeracki, M. (2019) *Understanding How We Learn: A Visual Guide*. London: Routledge.

Wiliam, D. (2011) *Embedded Formative Assessment*. Bloomington, IN: Solution Tree Press.

Wiliam, D. (2018) *Creating the Schools Our Children Need: Why What We're Doing Now Won't Help Much (And What We Can Do Instead)*. West Palm Beach, FL: Learning Sciences International.

Willingham, D.T. (2009) *Why Don't Students Like School? A Cognitive Scientist Answers Questions About How the Mind Works and What it Means for the Classroom*. San Francisco, CA: Jossey-Bass.

Acknowledgements

Writing and publishing a book is a team effort, and the support I have had with *Power Up Your Questioning* has been outstanding.

I would like to start by thanking everyone at John Catt Educational from Hachette Learning for everything they have done to support me. This includes Alex Sharratt for commissioning the book, Natasha Gladwell for her excellent work with proofreading and editing, and Gary Kilpatrick for everything he did with graphics to make *Power Up Your Questioning* look so good.

Next, I would like to thank everyone who has spent time reading advance copies of *Power Up Your Questioning* and contributing to it. Dylan Wiliam wrote a brilliant foreword, for which I am extremely grateful. Testimonials have been written by Rob Coe, John Hattie, Carl Hendrick, Lindsay Paterson, Kate Jones and Patrice Bain – quite the list of educational superstars! I really appreciate the support of all of them and am delighted by the praise they have given the book. It means a great deal.

Finally, I would like to thank a number of family and friends. These include my mum, for all her support in the background, my friend Derek Huffman for the time he has spent – as always – reading early drafts and offering helpful advice, and my husband, Jamie, for the incredible support he offers every day and his unwavering positivity.

What a team!

Together we unlock every learner's unique potential

At Hachette Learning (formerly Hodder Education), there's one thing we're certain about. No two students learn the same way. That's why our approach to teaching begins by recognising the needs of individuals first.

Our mission is to allow every learner to fulfil their unique potential by empowering those who teach them. From our expert teaching and learning resources to our digital educational tools that make learning easier and more accessible for all, we provide solutions designed to maximise the impact of learning for every teacher, parent and student.

Aligned to our parent company, Hachette Livre, founded in 1826, we pride ourselves on being a learning solutions provider with a global footprint.

www.hachettelearning.com